A CENTURY OF FELLS

NATIONAL PONY SOCIETY STUD BOOK

Volume V

Fell Committee

Mr. W. W. Wingate-Saul, Fenton Cawthorne House, Lancaster.
Mr. Robert W. Gibson, Orton, Tebay, Westmorland.
Mr. William Graham, Eden Grove, Kirkby Thore, Penrith.
Mr. R. M. Malloch, Kirkby Stephen, Westmorland.

As regards the characteristics of the Fell Pony, Mr. W. W. Wingate-Saul says:–

A very powerful and compact cobby build, the majority having a strong middle piece with deep chest and strong loin-characteristics, which, combined with deep sloping shoulders and fine withers, make them essentially weight-carrying riding ponies. The prevailing – indeed the only colours are black, brown, bay and quite occasionally grey. I do not remember ever having seen a chestnut, and if I found one I should think it due to the introduction of other blood. The four colours prevail in the order named, the best animals often being jet black and usually without white markings unless it be a small white star. The head is pony-like and intelligent, with large bright eyes and well-placed ears. The neck in the best examples being long enough to give a good rein to the rider. The hind quarters are square and strong with a well set-on tail. The legs have more bone than those of any of our indigenous breeds, ponies under 14 hands often measuring 8½ inches below the knee. Their muscularity of arm, thigh, and second thigh is marvellous.

Their habitat (having been bred for centuries on the cold inhospitable Fells where they are still to be found), has caused a wonderful growth of hair, the winter coat being heavy and legs growing a good deal of fine hair, all of which, excepting some at the point of the heel, being cast in summer. Constitutionally they are hard as iron, with good all-round action, and are very fast and enduring.

Stallions

BROUGH HILL 159. Bay. Foaled 1894. Height 13-2.
  S: Blooming Heather (Fell).
  D: Fell Pony.
  O: Lords A. and L. Cecil, Orchardmains, Tonbridge, Kent.
  B: Gibson, Widdy Bank, Middleton-in-Teasdale, Co. Durham.

EDEN GROVE 160. Brown. Foaled 1894. Height 13-2.
  S: Blooming Heather (Fell).
  D: Fell Pony.
  O: Lords A. and L. Cecil, Orchardmains, Tonbridge, Kent.
  B: Gibson, Widdy Bank, Middleton-in-Teasdale, Co. Durham.

Mares

860 BESSIE Black, white star. Foaled 1895. Height 13-2½.
  O: John Loxam, Carus Farm, Halton, Lancaster.
  R: William Stamper, Little Asphey Moor, Appleby, Westmorland.

861 BROWN FANNY Brown. Foaled 1882. Height 13-1.
  O: R. W. Gibson, Orton, Tebay, R.S.O., Westmorland.

Prod. in	Colour	Sex	Breeder	Name of Produce	Sire's Name and Breeding
1898	Brown	C.	Owner	Dandy	Bene II (Hackney St.B.)

1

A CENTURY OF FELLS

MARKING 100 YEARS OF THE FELL PONY SOCIETY

1922-2022

Sue Millard

Jackdaw E Books 2022
www.jackdawebooks.co.uk

FELL PONY SOCIETY

THE FPS COUNCIL 2022

Officers
President, Mrs SC Morton
Chairman, Mr Peter Boustead
Vice Chairman, Mr Paul Metcalfe
Secretary, Mrs Katherine Wilkinson
Treasurer, Mrs Elizabeth Parkin

Council, March 2022
Alison Bell
Peter Boustead
Rachael Brunskill
Sarah Charlton
Glenis Cockbain
Ruth Eastwood
Michael Goddard
Barry Mallinson
Paul Metcalfe
Sue Millard
Bill Potter
John Potter
Colin Roberts
Jane Rawden
Christine Robinson
Claire Simpson
Di Slack
Andrew Thorpe
Eileen Walker
David Wilkinson

DEDICATION

To Her Majesty Queen Elizabeth II
in the year of her Platinum Jubilee
1952-2022
Patron of the Fell Pony Society 1982-2022

A Century of Fells, Copyright © 2022 Susan Millard

ISBNs:
978-1-913106-17-1 (Hardback)
978-1-913106-16-4 (Paperback)
978-1-913106-18-1 (E-book)

Published by Jackdaw E Books, Greenholme, Cumbria CA10 3TA, UK
Edited by Sue Millard

Contributors
Clive Richardson
John Cockbain; Jenifer Morrissey;
Victoria Tollman; Eileen Walker; Liz Whitley

Cover Art by Sue Millard
Cover image sources: FW Garnett; Charlton Collection;
Michael Goddard; 1st Class Images; Lucy Jones; Sue Millard.

A CENTURY OF FELLS

THE FELL PONY is the heritage horse breed of North-West England, and its roots go back to pre-history. Descended from the fast, enduring Galloway stock mentioned by Shakespeare, the Fell pony became known by its modern name around 1853. From being a hardy farm worker, a tough military mount and pack-horse, a foundation breed for the upper-class recreation of polo, and a tradesman's pony in town, by the 1950s it had been adopted as a fun ride-and-drive for all the family, resilient, friendly, clever and easy to keep.

THE FELL PONY SOCIETY was founded in its present form in 1922. This book celebrates its Centenary with sequenced photographs of many families of ponies recorded in the Stud Book through the years. It also prompts consideration of how the breed may develop in the next century.

Scrapbook copy of the FPS Report of 1952: Ponies on the Arnside Stallion Enclosure in 1950.

Scrapbook Article by "S.H.C." - date uncertain, possibly late 1940s/early 1950s. The author (perhaps Sylvia Hasell-McCosh?) refers to "our parish fells and commons at Caldbeck" so the newspaper is probably Penrith-based, eg Penrith Observer or Cumberland & Westmorland Herald. Both Photos, courtesy of Mr AW Morland

Contents

FELL PONY CHAMPION AT PENRITH

"Guards Model" owned and bred by Mr. Richard Little, Guards, Ireby, which won the Lady Yule Cup for the best stallion or colt at the Fell Pony Society's annual show of registered ponies at Penrith on Tuesday.

Photo : Hardman, Kendal

Guards Model, owned and bred by Mr Richard Little, Ireby, won the Championship at the Stallion Show at Penrith; probably in 1957 although the stallion also won this award in 1965 and 1967. Photo, Joseph Hardman, probably in the Westmorland Gazette. *Courtesy of Mr AW Morland.*

Introduction

The FPS Centenary 1922-2022

In 2022 the Fell Pony Society celebrates the official centenary of its founding: 100 years of looking after the interests of the Fell ponies of the North of England. For the majority of that time, the work was done unsalaried, as a labour of love. Now the Secretary and her assistant are paid a wage, and the Webmaster and the Show Secretary receive an honorarium, but everyone else on the FPS Council, including the Chairman, still works on a volunteer basis.

The story of the Fell pony breed does not start a hundred years ago – far from it. Even the story of the Society itself starts well before 1922. For an excellent account of the Fell Pony breed up to 1990 I recommend Clive Richardson's *The Fell Pony*, while for the early history it is also useful to read *Dales Ponies* by Iona Fitzgerald, since the two breeds come from the same root and they remained strongly intertwined until the closure of the Stud Books.

What I hope to do in this book is threefold:

- to display photographs of ponies, male and female, famous and not so famous, in the context of their pedigrees and photographs of their progeny;
- to add archive information that has come to light since 1990;
- to include a brief overview of what the Society has done in the 30+ years since then.

I do not intend to re-hash here the family histories of Fell pony studs which have already been given in books such as RB Charlton's *A Lifetime With Ponies,* or by Bert and Carole Morland in *A Lifetime in the Fells* and *A Walk on the Wild Side*, or by my own *Hoofprints in Eden*. All except *A Lifetime in the Fells* are available from the Society.

Also, there will inevitably be gaps. For instance, I have not been able to find images of the oldest ponies said to be part of the breed, such as Lingcropper, a remnant from the Scots army after the 1745 uprising, who was probably a Galloway; and I have not looked for any Hackneys, roadsters, Clydesdales or cobs whose names occur singly as sires in the oldest registrations. I had more than enough illustrative material from the 1900s onward to fill my original "Century" plan for 100 pages, and despite more than doubling that, what I have included is only a set of examples, some good, some less good, showing how the breed has been maintained up to 2022. The original photographic material itself is variable - from newspaper clippings to professional portraits - so please excuse some of the historic images lacking quality. I have transcribed parts of newspaper articles where I had space to do so.

There is a bibliography at the end of this book to acknowledge the sources I've used. That should help other Fell pony enthusiasts to find useful information about the breed, such as archives, collections, books, museums and web sites.

Any factual or data errors are mine. If you find something wrong let me know, privately, and I will correct them in the next edition.

Sue Millard, 2022

Coronation Report
of

The Fell Pony Society

OCTOBER 1951 ———— MARCH 1954

FELL PONIES ABOVE MARTINDALE.

Penrith :
Reed's Ltd., Printers, etc.

1954.

The cover of the Coronation Report of the Fell Pony Society in 1954, in the FPS archive, Cumbria County Archives, Kendal. Reed's are still the printers of the FPS Magazine.

A BRIEF HISTORY

BEFORE THEY WERE FELLS
Sue Millard

Pre-history

Archaeological records tell us that equines existed in Britain before the Ice Ages, but the changing climate that brought permanent snow cover must have forced them to move south. During that time, when glaciers and ice sheets scoured the landscape to form the characteristic landscapes of the Scottish Highlands, Lake District and North Wales, the ice would have been hundreds of metres thick. It reached as far south as London. The climate immediately beyond the ice would also have been very inhospitable – worse than the Cairngorms in winter – so the ancient ponies, along with other wild fauna and with early humans, could only live well by moving to the warmer European landmass to the south.

The English Channel had formed relatively early (~180,00 years ago) but when the ice began to retreat after the last glacial maximum, much of the water was still frozen, so a land connection between Britain and Europe would have existed; a river valley in the Channel area and, in the southern North Sea between Lincolnshire, East Anglia and Holland, now referred to as the Doggerland, there were marshes, low hills and pasture.

With the gradual thaw there would have been a pattern of regrowth, from shoreline and wetland plants, to mosses, lichens, sedges, reeds and open grassland, to scrub, trees and woodland. During that period, both animals and people could migrate between Britain and Europe, and archaeologists are cautious about saying whether ponies were re-introduced to Britain by humans, or arrived independently; it was possible for both to migrate across the Doggerland, the animals probably spreading from the south east of England to Wales, northern England, Scotland and Ireland.

However, around 6,200 BCE a huge underwater landslide off the coast of Norway triggered a tsunami that flooded the Doggerland and the Channel. With further climate warming and sea levels continuing to rise, by about 5,500 BCE Britain had become the group of islands we know now. (Gaffney et al, 2007). After that, the animal population of Britain was isolated from that of Europe and any new genetic material can only have been introduced by human activity such as migration, trade and warfare.

So, for the best part of 7 millennia, the ponies and horses of the British Isles have been separate from those on the European mainland. This is not to say that our native breeds would have looked then exactly as they do today. In European horses, in the Copper Age, coat colours at first were bay or bay/dun, joined before 4,000 BCE by black. By 2,000 BCE (Bronze Age) chestnut, tobiano and sabino were present; by the Iron Age buckskin and black-silver had appeared (Ludwig et al, 2009). However, the foundation of British breeds must have come from the oldest, isolated section of that population, so most of the animals were likely to have been bay, bay/dun or black.

Roman Occupation

We know a lot about the uses of horses (and ponies, not forgetting oxen, donkeys and mules) from sculptures, mosaics and tombstone inscriptions. Riders needed horses both in peacetime and war. Chariots required ponies and horses to pull them. There are accounting records, from the Roman fort of Vindolanda on Hadrian's Wall, of pack-saddle covers being paid for, so we know there were pack-saddles and therefore there were pack-horses. Wagons and farm implements may have been drawn by horses, mules, or oxen.

All these animals were selected for their various tasks by experience and observation. Virgil's *Georgics*, for instance, advises on the ages at which cattle and horses are most fertile and most useful as workers on the farm. "Whether a man aspires to the prize of Olympia's palm and breeds horses, or rears bullocks, strong for the plough, let his chief care be to choose the mould of the dams." His poetry talks about the colours of cattle and the desirable appearance of a good horse, and how to rear a foal well:

> Only, upon those whom you mean to rear for the hope of the race, be sure to spend special pains, even from their early youth. … From the first, the foal of a noble breed steps higher in the fields and brings down his feet lightly. Boldly he leads the way, braves threatening rivers, entrusts himself to an untried bridge, and starts not at idle sounds. His neck is high, his head clean-cut, his belly short, his back plump, and his gallant chest is rich in muscles. Good colours are bay and grey; the worst, white and dun. Again, should he but hear afar the clash of arms, he cannot keep his place; he pricks up his ears, quivers his limbs, and snorting rolls beneath his nostrils the gathered fire. His mane is thick and, as he tosses it, falls back on his right shoulder. A double ridge runs along his loins; when his hoof scoops out the ground, the solid horn makes a deep ring.

Virgil advises the farmer to "select the mother's stock carefully" both for cattle and horses. He doesn't, however, identify the foals of a "noble" line by anything we would recognise as a "breed" name. Also, although various classical authors discuss the value of horses from certain areas of the Middle East for racing and warfare, none of the literature I've read mentions pedigree choices being made in Britain when breeding domestic animals. "Pedigrees" as we know them were not being recorded. The concept of a closed stud book and a "breed" of livestock is a relatively modern one dating from the 18th century, eg, the General Stud Book of the Thoroughbred racehorse founded in 1791. Before then, all that was wanted was a horse that could do a job.

Although there are references to horses being bought by the Roman Army and heavy cavalry horses being produced in Lancashire (Davies, 1969), we know very little about their breeding.

Post-Roman and medieval period

Once the Roman military presence had been withdrawn from Britain, around 410AD, only the richest individuals could afford to import stock to Britain from overseas to improve the animals they bred. Given the expense and the effort involved they would probably have reserved them for their own use. Such imported blood may not have reached the wider gene pool until many generations later, if at all, so any exotic influence on the ponies running wild, or owned by "Joe Public", is likely to have been small.

Descriptive names for types of horses indicate what they did, or what they looked like, or how they moved:

courser (galloping horse for hunting or racing),

rouncy (trotting cob with diagonal gaits),

haquenee (hack for travelling),

sumpter (pack-horse),

destrier (knight's fighting war horse, a trotting horse),

ambling pad (horse with easy lateral gaits),

nag (general riding horse).

The British horse and pony breeds have accumulated plenty of mythical "ancient origin" stories: from Roman imports to Andalucian survivors of the Spanish Armada. I have not found any contemporary text to support any of them. It isn't until we reach the end of the 16th century that a name emerges that deserves our attention with regard to the Fell pony: and that is the "Galloway nag".

THE GALLOWAY NAG

Late 16th to 17th Century

The earliest reference I know (at present) to the Galloway is in a letter of 1584 from Archbishop Adamson of St Andrews, Scotland, to Queen Elizabeth I's Secretary Walsingham, asking for a favour and offering to make Walsingham a present of "a Galloway nag". A more widely known one is in Shakespeare's Henry IV part II (1597), where Falstaff's sidekick "Ancient Pistol", described as a "swaggering rascal", makes advances towards Doll Tearsheet using horsey analogies, claiming that he is superior to "packhorses, and hollow pampered jades of Asia that cannot go but thirty miles a day." She scorns him, however:

"For God's sake, thrust him down stairs: I cannot endure such a fustian rascal."

At which Pistol shouts back:

"'Thrust him down stairs!'? know we not Galloway nags?"

Shakespeare clearly expected the 1597 audience to understand the various types of horse that Pistol compares himself to. After that date, the term Galloway can be found regularly in print.

Gervase Markham, The Compleat Horseman: 1607

"Also in Scotland there are a race of small nagges which they call Galloways or Galloway nagges which for fine shape, easie pace, pure metall and infinit toughness are not short of the best nagges that are bred in any country whatsoever."

16

Britannia, 1607

Camden, the dogged traveller of Elizabeth's reign, wrote of Galloways as "tiny horses with compact, strong limbs for enduring toil."

Defoe's Tour Through Scotland

Defoe (1660-1731) wrote of Galloways:

> "...they have the best breed of strong low horses in Britain, if not in Europe, which we call pads, and from whence we call all small truss-strong riding horses Galloways. These horses are remarkable for being good pacers, strong, easy goers, hardy, gentle, well broke, and above all, that they never tire, and they are very much bought up in England on that account."

In the Westmorland county archives at the end of the 17thC a butcher and a mason living in Brough were each recorded as owning a Galloway; one was worth £2, and the other only 5 shillings.

18th Century - Exporting Galloways

John Spreull (1646-1722), known as "Bass John", wrote in 1706 that he bought and sold "fine Scots galloway horses". He stated:

> "Search the custom books at Port Glasgow where I myself entered and payed [export] dutie for 50 or 52 mostly ston'd horses and maers which I shipped in a great ship of 400 Tunn for Surinam an Dutch Plantation for a brood of horses, and they were almost all Highland Galloways excepting some few ...

> "And for certaintie the borderers on both Scots and English side came oft to Dunbarton fair and bought small droves of them when they carried up their cattle. And what gentleman did ever ride post in any or all of the roads of England and never met with a Scots galloway? if they have not, I am sure I have, and I have frequented the roads there ... and still when I had some Scots galloway it was coveted and often bought from me. And I can aver as a truth that an Scots galloway of 40 or 50 shils ster [sterling] per piece will ride farder and kill and beat and founder an English Geldin of 20, 30, 40 or 50 £ ster price. ...

> "I know them ride 40 or 50 miles a day; and then they are kept easilie and can feed upon the Orts [leftovers] of others. It's true English Geldings 30, 40, or 50 £ ster price may run [gallop], and course [race] and do wonders, yet I shall kill them with a Scots galloway of 40, 50 shil or 5 £ ster price, through long fatigue and [the] time, scarcity and wants incident."

Spreull gives us a dealer's view of the Galloway: cheap, hardy and enduring. In Scotland semi-feral herds of them seem to have lived on the hill in large numbers. (Bibby, 2022, *pers. comm.*) The Galloway is to be met with everywhere; he is strong and infinitely useful; but he is a Land Rover rather than a Ferrari.

Stolen! - Newcastle Courant, Sat 20 Oct 1711

"... a dark Gray Colt Galloway, 12 hands high, with a short Bob-Tail, past Four Years Old : give Notice [...] to Thomas Drinkrow... "

Alexander Pope, 1713

"The Guardian," No 91, June 25, 1713 Volume 2, published a Letter by Alexander Pope, detailing the comical Rules of "The Short Club, a Society of Men who dare to be short".

"III If any member shall purchase a horse for his own riding above fourteen hands and an half in height, that horse shall forthwith be sold, a Scotch galloway bought in its stead for him, and the overplus of the money shall treat the club."

We can infer from this that Galloways were cheap, and under 14.2 hands.

Penrith Races in Cumberland, 1736

ON Wednesday the 16th Day of June next, will be run for on the usual Course on Maidenhill, a Purse of 15 Guineas, by any Horse, &c. not exceeding five Years old this Grass, to be certify'd for; three Heats, each Heat 3 Miles; five Year olds to carry 9 Stone, four year olds 8 Stone; One Guinea and a half Entrance.

On Thursday the 17th Day of June, will be run for a Purse of 8 Guineas by Galloways, 14 Hands to carry 9 Stone, all under to have the usual Abatement; three Heats, each Heat 4 Miles; Fifteen Shillings Entrance.

Appleby Races, 1736

On Thursday, Friday, and Saturday, being the First, Second, and Third Days of July, will be run for on Brampton Moor near Appleby in Westmoreland, three Purses of Gold of Ten, Five, and Twelve Guineas, raised by Subscription, and run in Manner following.

THE first Ten Guineas given by Walter Plummer and John Ramsden, Esqrs. Members for the said Borough, on Thursday the First of July, by Galloways, 14 Hands carrying 10 Stone, and Weight for Inches over and under, 4 miles to a Heat.

On Friday Five Guineas, by Ponies, 13 Hands carrying 9 Stone, Weight for Inches under, 4 Miles to a Heat.

On Saturday Twelve Guineas, give and take, 14 Hands carrying 10 Stone, weight for Inches over and under, 4 Miles to a Heat.

Horses vs. Galloways vs. Ponies

The various 18thC race-day advertisements distinguish between horses (14 hands), Galloways (14 hands), ponies (13 hands) and hunters. Since the horses and the Galloways were frequently of the same height and set to carry the same range of weight it is interesting to speculate as to the difference between them. Was it simply one of pedigree, or was it the gait at which they were raced? Were horses expected to gallop and Galloways to trot or pace? There are references to Galloways that might be interpreted as having lateral gaits (Markham and Defoe remark on "easy paces") but others that might be diagonal gaits (Morgan had observed a hundred years before Defoe that "Scotland excels in trotting geldings").

An advertisement in the *Caledonian Mercury*, 19 April 1739, listed for auction "a Pac'd Galloway". The fact that the term "pac'd" was added not only implies that this particular Galloway did indeed pace, but that the attribute needed to be mentioned as otherwise buyers would assume it was a square trotter. The same pattern shows up in transactions in the Appleby Minute Book *[Cumbria County Archives, Kendal]*, where occasional sales of racking or pacing horses are described as such, while many other are not and can be assumed to be diagonal gaited.

Nathan Bailey's *Dictionarium Brittanicum: or A More Compleat Universal Etymological English Dictionary* (1730s) defines the word pony as "a little Scotch horse". The Galloway was defined by Dr Johnson in his 1755 Dictionary as "a horse not more than fourteen hands high, much used in the North; probably as coming originally from Galloway, a shire in Scotland."

As a type the name "galloway" soon became transferred to other small horses, lost its capital letter and became a generic noun in the same way that "hoover" has become synonymous with "vacuum cleaner". Accounts of the Fell pony breed from quite early on have retained the understanding that the now-extinct Galloway nag is the ancestor of at least three British pony breeds, the Highland, the Dales, and the Fell.

Galloways as racehorse ancestors

It is sometimes forgotten, when discussing the foundation sires of the thoroughbred, that the Darley Arabian, Byerley Turk, Godolphin Arabian & Co could not reproduce themselves in a vacuum! Quite apart from there being many more imported stallions than these three, and that most were Turkoman, Akhal-Teke or Barb rather than Arabian, they were crossed onto British mares such as the Galloways. Modern research seems to support this hypothesis. (Bower, 2010; Hardiman, 2013). The "speed gene" in sprinters traces back to a native British mare.

The Curwen family of West Cumbria bred horses for races similar to those in the advertisements previously mentioned; the animals were still known by the "Galloway" name, for instance the Curwen Galloway, an ancestor of the great stallion Eclipse from whom many racing sires descended, such as Shergar and Mill Reef. This is a debt owed by the Thoroughbred to the Galloway stock. The purpose-bred racing "Galloways" had been derived from the native Galloway nag by several generations of breeding to Oriental sires. Still, by maternal descent our modern Fells, Dales and Highlands are still cousins, many-times-removed, of today's racing Thoroughbreds.

Agricultural Surveys, 1794

Scotsman Andrew Pringle, writing a Report about Westmorland for the Board of Agriculture in 1794, noted that "The Commons are numerous, extensive and valuable ..." and added that they were mainly stocked with Scotch sheep, black cattle and geese. He observed frustratingly briefly that "a few ponies of the Scotch breed are reared upon the commons, but the practice not being general, need not be dilated upon."

He distinguished between these "ponies" and the local "horses", which he did not consider particularly useful or valuable; he did not seem to think it necessary to explain the term "Scotch pony", which suggests it was in common use and widely understood. It seems reasonable to assume it was the same as the Galloway, since Tuke, writing in the same national survey about the North Riding of Yorkshire, uses "Scotch" alongside "Galloway", just as Pope had done 80 years before.

> "Horses constitute a considerable part of the stock of the high parts of the western moorlands; the farmers there generally keep a few Scotch Galloways, which they put to stallions of the country, and produce a hardy and very strong race in proportion to their size, which are chiefly sold to the manufacturing part of the West Riding and Lancashire, to be employed in ordinary purposes."

It's also notable that both surveyors use the same quantifier, "a few" Scotch Galloways, "a few" ponies of the Scotch breed – not "many". Pringle says plainly that rearing ponies on the open fell was not widespread: "the practice not being general". It would have depended, then as now, on the pony owner having a "right" on the common. The rights, remaining from very early times, were becoming increasingly restricted as the various Enclosure Acts were passed, which permitted the open fields and large tracts of common land to be divided into various parcels, walled or hedged. Individuals or institutions were "allotted" these parcels of land and gained legal property rights over them even though the land was previously held "in common" and available to everyone in the village. Between 1604 and 1914, over 5,200 Acts were put into place, enclosing 6.8 million acres, and the common lands shrank inside a circle of allotments. (There is a further, detailed chapter on the Fell Commons coming up later.) Some of the surveyors for the Board of Agriculture were definitely pushing for further enclosure and improvement of the commons; Pringle, by contrast, seems to have reported without bias.

Pony breeding on the hill farms may have involved only one or two mares per farm, rather than a herd. That would agree with the word "few". For instance, two mares breeding a foal in alternate years could be useful on the farm and productive in terms of saleable offspring. The mare who foaled last year would do the work on the farm this year and go to the stallion to foal next year. If the foal was sold in the autumn, that left only the two mares to keep over winter, and they might even have lived most of the year on rough corners of the farm, without needing turnout on the commons. However, if the foals were retained to a usable age, a mare with this year's foal at foot would have with her the other mare's yearling, her own 2-year-old, and possibly the other mare's 3-year-old - a little herd of five for which a common right would have been very helpful to a small farm that was relying on its in-bye grassland to rear sheep and cattle, and provide hay for winter.

The actual numbers of each type of horse in Cumbria and North Yorkshire are not included in the 1794 Reports because Pringle and Tuke et al. were contributing to a general survey of farming practices, rather than a census. However, from the sparse nature of their remarks about ponies, and the fact that they discuss horses separately, we can deduce that ponies were not used enough in farming to be worth recording. There are probably more Fell ponies alive now than the "few" Scotch ponies recorded at the end of the 18th century.

William Hutchinson's *History of the County of Cumberland*, 1794, describes galloways being used to carry coal from the pits to the ships in Whitehaven harbour:

> "The coals were then drawn out of the pits by men with jack-rowls, or windlasses, and were carried from the pits to the ships by galloways or small horses, upon their backs in packs, weighing about fourteen stone each, and measuring about three Winchester bushels, or twenty-four gallons. There is a print of Whitehaven extant, in which is exhibited a man driving some of these galloways, with packs of coals on their backs, towards the ships."

Scottish Parish Surveys, 1790 --

On the Scottish side of the Border, Parish surveys were also conducted between 1791 and 1799, in which it was noted: from Twynholme (Kirkcudbright, Galloway region):

> "The old breed of Galloways, so highly valued for spirit and shape ... is almost entirely, if not totally extinct."

Heltondale ponies coming down off the fell after heavy snow, March 1995. Photo, Mrs Greta Noble.

THE 19TH CENTURY
Sue Millard

The Agriculture of Galloway

Rev. Sam. Smith's survey, *General View of the Agriculture of Galloway*, was published in 1810.

"SECT. IV. HORSES.

"...in former times, when the inhabitants were engaged in constant predatory warfare, greater value would be attached to animals so very light and active, peculiarly adapted to climb over high and rugged mountains, and to endure fatigue, cold and hunger in a very great degree. From the hardships they had to undergo, none but such as were thriving and hardy would survive till they reached maturity. And the breed being thus constantly purged of all those of less hardy constitutions, would attain to that excellence for which it has been justly praised. It cannot be denied, however, that such of the true Galloways as still remain, resemble the Spanish horses in some very characteristic features, particularly in their faces. This similarity makes it very probable, that although the breed of Galloways be not indebted for its origin, yet it has received material improvement from such a circumstance as has been mentioned.

"It is much to be regretted that this ancient breed is now almost lost. This has been occasioned chiefly by the desire of farmers to breed horses of greater weight, and better adapted for the draught; and from the little value attached, in times of tranquillity, to horses well calculated for predatory excursions.

"...Those which have a considerable portion of the old blood are easily distinguished by smallness of head and neck, and cleanness of bone, not usual in draught horses. They are generally of a light bay or brown, and their legs black."

Parts of this text can also be found almost word-for-word in other books, eg Youatt's *The Horse* (1831 and reprints). Since neither of them credits the other I can only go by the publication dates, in which case Smith's survey was the original. In both, the terms "clean legs" and "clean bone" are used. "Clean" meant the flat, flinty quality of bone we see in a good Fell or Dales pony today. It doesn't necessarily mean that the legs carried no feather. A small amount of hair at the point of the fetlock – "footlocks" – can be seen in many old illustrations of British horses, and was probably a characteristic of all the native stock.

"...over all the ancient wastes and forests of England, formerly covering the larger part of the surface of the country, were reared varieties of horses, the size and strength of which bore a relation to the quality and abundance of the natural herbage. Sometimes they were of the pony size, falling short of twelve hands high; sometimes they reached fourteen hands, and in rarer cases fifteen. They were of coarse form, with short hairy limbs, and were capable of much drudgery, but were destitute of elegance, and unsuited for speed. From this class were derived the older Pack-horses, which were used throughout the country before roads were formed, and which, until late in the last century, were the most numerous class of horses employed ... hardy and sure-footed, but wanted action and lightness for the saddle ...

"A variety of horses, differing from the ordinary pack-horses in their greater lightness and elegance of figure, were termed Galloways. They exceeded the pony size, and were greatly valued for their activity and bottom [stamina]. They were derived from the countries near the Solway Firth..." [*On the domesticated animals of the British islands*, David Low, 1846]

Separately, Low also mentions the Connemara pony as retaining "the peculiar amble of the Spanish Jennet." He does not mention this about the Galloway, so perhaps he was aware that any lateral gaits of the type had by then been lost.

Peepings, 1820

The Dargue family Bible records that Thomas Dargue of Bow Hall married Anne Shepherd of Murton Hall on 6th June 1820. Anne brought with her a dowry of twenty grey Galloways. This is so far the oldest record from a family who are still breeding Fell ponies, and keeping them on the fell; they still use the "Peepings" prefix.

"Fell Pony" - Westmorland Gazette, October 1853

DENT ..... of so gifted a son.
HORSE FAIR. — At this old established fair which was held on Monday last, the show of Fell ponies was better both in quantity and quality, than it has been for a year or two back. The prices realized for the ponies were upon the whole, considerably in advance of last year's prices.

Currently the first known use of the term "fell pony" comes in the Westmorland Gazette in 1853 (held by the British Library):

Dent is a village in the Dales, close to the boundary between Yorkshire and Westmorland. Reference in the newspaper to sales "a year or two back" suggests that "fell ponies" had been sold at this fair for some time previously.

Note the absence of a capital F, which suggests that the term "fell pony" was not yet a breed name: it was "a pony that has been living at the fell". This usage is very similar to the way that modern sheep breeds like Swaledales, Roughs and Herdwicks are grouped in conversation under the one term "fell sheep", or a working sheepdog with huge energy and stamina is complimented as "a good fell dog".

Stud Books

In 1893 the National Pony Society was founded "for the improvement and encouragement of the breeding of high class riding and polo ponies". The first entries of Fell ponies in this stud book were in 1898 when it opened sections for "British ponies of the mountain and moorland breeds", and each breed had a Committee to inspect ponies and look after the registrations. For the Fells this Committee consisted of Mr WW Wingate-Saul, Lancaster; Mr Robert W Gibson, Orton, Westmorland; Mr William Graham, Kirkby Thore, Cumberland; and Mr RM Malloch, Kirkby Stephen, Westmorland.

In this first description of the Fell Pony, Mr Wingate-Saul wrote:

"A very powerful and compact cobby build, the majority having a strong middle piece with deep chest and strong loin-characteristics, which, combined with deep sloping shoulders and fine withers, make them essentially weight-carrying riding ponies. The prevailing – indeed the only colours are black, brown, bay and quite occasionally grey. I do not remember ever having seen a chestnut, and if I found one I should think it due to the introduction of other blood. The four colours prevail in the order named, the best animals often being jet black and usually without white marking unless it be a small white star. The head is pony-like and intelligent, with large bright eyes and well-placed ears. The neck in the best examples being long enough to give a good rein to the rider. The hind quarters are square and strong with a well set-on tail. The legs have more bone than those of any of our indigenous breeds, ponies under 14 hands often measuring 8½ inches below the knee. Their muscularity of arm, thigh and second thigh is marvellous.

"Their habitat (having been bred for centuries on the cold inhospitable Fells where they are still to be found) has caused a wonderful growth of hair, the winter coat being heavy and legs growing a good deal of fine hair, all of which, excepting some at the point of the heel, being cast in summer. Constitutionally they are as hard as iron, with good all-round action, and are very fast and enduring."

The 19th century, then, closed with the Fell pony recognised by the National Pony Society. Nationally, it was thought of as a local type suitable for breeding polo ponies, but in its home country it had a small committee of supporters and breeders whose stated intention to preserve "the old breed" soon came to conflict with that.

THE 20TH CENTURY

Sue Millard

Sir Walter Gilbey, quoting Mr William Graham of Eden Grove, wrote in 1903: "Up to about fifty years ago great interest seems to have been taken in pony or galloway cob breeding throughout the whole district of the Eden valley, in the villages and hamlets that lie scattered all along the foot of the Pennine range of hills. Previous to the days of railway transit the ponies and small galloway cobs were employed in droves as pack-horses, as well as for riding, and many men now living can remember droves of from twenty to thirty continually travelling the district, carrying panniers of coal and other merchandise between the mines and the villages. ... An authority resident at Harrington who gives much information concerning the ponies of the Fell-side holdings and moors states that there are several strains, and the appearance and character of each differ in various districts under the various local influences of climate, feed, etc; little or nothing is known of the origin of these ponies."

In 1912 a Fell Pony Committee was set up by a group of breeders to look after the welfare, breeding and registration of Fell ponies. Its purposes were different from those of the early National Pony Society, in that it resisted the trend for "improvement" and the tendency to breed lighter ponies for sport. Its aim was "to keep pure the old breed that has roamed the fells for years." Mr Frank Garnett, president of the Royal College of Veterinary Surgeons, was a major force in the setting up of the Fell Pony Society. He worked towards it from 1903 until 1912, when he and Lord Lonsdale headed this newly formed Northern Committee.

This Fell Pony Committee for Cumberland, Westmorland and North Yorkshire in time became the Fell Pony Society. Frank Garnett was secretary to the Committee, and when the Fell Pony Society was forming, his office was transferred to that. The list of subsequent Secretaries and the Society's timeline are on p203.

1916

E de V Irving, Chairman,
Stonecroft, Shap

Dr RW Gibson, Vice Chairman,
Orton

G Norris Midwood, The Grange,
Congleton

M Bennett, Wallthwaite, Keswick

A Lawson, Hesket Hall, Wigton

J Hird, Snowhill, Caldbeck

J Bainbridge, Harcourt House,
Kirkby Stephen

E Handley, Park House,
Ravenstonedale

H Holme, Thrimby, Penrith

J Dargue, Bow Hall, Dufton

J Wills, Nether Hoff, Appleby

T Bainbridge Jr, Brough Castle,
Brough

R Sayer, Winton, K Stephen

JW Dent, Stanhopegate, Middleton

TW Beadle, Middleton

J Upton, Ingmire Hall,
Sedbergh

W Sedgwick, Thwaite,
Howgill

FW Garnett, Hon Secretary
& Treasurer

SUE MILLARD

The Fell Pony Committee
Earl of Lonsdale, President, Lowther Castle

Committee Meetings: The Minute Book
(Transcriptions and spellings as in the original text.)

8 March 1916, Station Hotel, K Stephen (FP Committee)

4 - Secretary read a letter from Board of Agriculture agreeing to the committee's request to co-opt two additional members. The following were elected and have agreed to act, viz: Mr J Metcalfe, Heltondale; Mr R Dent, Warcop.

30 November 1916, Crown Hotel, Penrith (FP Committee)

Continue Stallion Premium scheme but preclude award of premium to a pony to travel for more than 4 consecutive seasons in the same district.

Selected ponies had been sent to the London Show, expenses paid by G Norris Midwood, Lord Lonsdale giving a premium of £4.4.0.

Balance sheet adopted for period 31 Dec 1914 to Jan (possibly June?) 31st 1916.

RB Charlton of Queens Letch, Hexham-on-Tyne, had written to propose the formation of a Dales Pony Society; Secretary instructed to write and inform him as to the Fell Pony Committee and the National Pony Society and the work they were and had been doing in the interests of Pony breeding.

9 March 1917, Station Hotel, K Stephen (FP Committee)

Stallion premiums received from Board of Agriculture.

Dates of stallion shows set for Appleby, K Stephen, Middleton, Keswick and Shap, judges appointed.

27 Nov 1917, Crown Hotel, Penrith (FP Committee)

On the discussion of the Report (of the National Pony Society? Or board of Agriculture?) proposed that no amalgamation between the Fell & Dales Society should take place at the present time and no objection to them entering in the Dales section ponies already entered in the Fell Section - the numbers to be as first entered.

Mr H Holme gave notice that he would move "That a horse by a registered sire out of a registered dam be eligible for entry in the Stud Book irrespective of height."

5 March 1918, Crown Hotel, Penrith (A meeting of the SOCIETY)

Proposed that one Show be held at K Stephen for the 3 Districts Appleby, K Stephen and Middleton on Monday April 22nd.

26 Nov 1918, Crown Hotel, Penrith (A meeting of the Society)

4 March 1919, Crown Hotel, Penrith (A meeting of the Society)

Where a stallion whose percentage of foals taken on the average of two seasons does not exceed a percentage of 40 to mares covered - the Society shall refuse the entry of such Stallions at their Shows for the award of the Breeds Premiums [see April 1921 re Tuer's Spring].

25 Nov 1919, Crown Hotel, Penrith

Resolved to advise the Royal Agricultural Society that a class for yearlings would take place.

24 Feb 1920, Crown Hotel, Penrith

5 stallion shows arranged plus judges.

23 Nov 1920, Crown Hotel, Penrith

The Society would send a group of ponies to the Spring NPS Show in London.

Stallions Dalesman and Glengarry will not be allowed to compete for the Ministry Premiums in the Appleby or Shap Districts in consequence of the number of years they have both travelled those Districts.

21 Dec 1920 at Penrith

Committee appointed to choose ponies for the NPS Group class at London show in Feb 1921.

8 Feb 1921, Crown Hotel, Penrith

Agreed to charge a subscription of 5/- per annum for membership of the Society.

Sec instructed to try and arrange a sale of Fell Ponies at K Stephen on Cowper Day, Sept 29th.

Ponies selected for the London Show were Lord Lonsdale's Hoo-Poe, Mr Watson's Baggra-Yeat Bella and Mr Allison's Nancy VII.

18 April 1921, 11-45am at Mr Bainbridge's office in Kirkby Stephen

Prizes agreed for two classes of ponies in the Sale - yearlings, 2 yr olds, champion class for the best Fell pony in the sale 4 yrs old or under and shown in hand. "The Fell Pony Society to appoint the judges and the Auction Company to advertise and take all risks." Secretary to write to the Dales Society to have classes at the Sale on Similar lines.

Fell pony stallion at Rough Hill, Bampton, March 1909.
Photo from FW Garnett's 'Westmorland Agriculture', 1912

28

Letter considered from Ministry of Agriculture regarding the foaling returns of "Tuers Spring" & it was recommended that the Ministry be advised not to award another Premium to this Stallion, he only having returned 3 (three) living foals from 36 mares & 2 other mares dead in foal.

22 Nov 1921, Crown Hotel, Penrith

Recommend that Ministry of Agriculture pay the Balance of Premium to "Hilton Passion"'s owner.

Letter from the Shire Horse Society to nominate a member of the Fell Pony Society to act on the Joint Parliamentary Committee of all the Horse and Pony Breeding Societies. Mr Garnett nominated.

Classes for mare with foal at foot and mare in foal to be offered at the Shows. Height of Fell ponies in future to be - Mares not exceeding 13-2 hands, Stallions not exceeding 14 hands; to be confirmed at the next meeting of the Society.

14 March 1922, Crown Hotel, Penrith

Proposed that Premium pony stallions be prohibited from serving Clydesdale or half-bred mares and that all mares served by a Premium stallion be of the Fell Pony Type – or approaching a pony type & not exceeding the height of the recognised native pony breeds. Carried unanimously.

Fell yearlings and 2 year olds at Rough Hill, Bampton, in March 1909. At the time, there were ponies registered by Henry Mattinson, High Roughhill, and George Mawson, Low Roughhill, so these ponies may have belonged to either.

Photo from FW Garnett's 'Westmorland Agriculture', 1912

THE FELL PONY SOCIETY

Minute Book

10 October, 1922, Crown Hotel, Penrith

Minutes of the Fell Pony Society, 10 October 1922

A meeting was held at the Crown Hotel, Penrith on Tuesday the 10th of October 1922.

Present. Mr E de Vere Irving in the Chair. Messrs H Watson, H Holme, J G Marston, J Bellas, F Watson, H Brown, A Lawson, Dr R W Gibson acting as Hon Sec & Treas. pro tem.

1. The minutes of the previous meeting were read, confirmed and signed by the Chairman.

2. Mr E de V Irving moved, Mr Holme seconded, a resolution that an expression of sympathy be conveyed by the Secretary to Mrs Garnett & family with reference to the death of the Hon Secy & Treasurer Mr F W Garnett. The resolution was passed, all the members and reporters present standing.

3. Resolved that an application be made for two Classes for Fell ponies at the Royal Show to be held at Newcastle in 1923, viz one stallion class and one mare class and that the Committee contribute the sum of Eighteen pounds to the prize fund for the said Classes.

4. Resolved that the present Committee be dissolved with the object of forming a Fell pony Society – and co-opting additional members to the committee – and the Election of Officers for the Ensuing years.

Confirmed and signed.

October 10 1922

A General meeting was held at the Crown Hotel Penrith after the preceding meeting to Consider the formation of a Fell pony Society –

Present. Mr E de Vere Irving in the Chair. Messrs H Watson, H Holme, J G Marston, J Bellas, F Watson, H Brown, A Lawson, Roy B Charlton, Major McKenzie, Captain Wingate, W J Wharton, J Relph, Dr R W Gibson acting as Secretary & Treasurer pro tem.

1. Resolved and carried unanimously that a Fell pony Society be formed and that the annual subscription for a member of the said Society be five Shillings.

2. Resolved that the Earl of Lonsdale be Elected Life President of the Society and that E de V Irving and G Norris Midwood Esquires be Elected vice-presidents.

3. Resolved that the members of the old Committee together with the representatives of the nominating Agricultural Societies and Messrs Roy B Charlton and J Relph constitute the new Council or Committee.

4. Capt Wingate on being asked to undertake the duties of the Hon. Secretary and Treasurer consented to do so with the temporary assistance of Dr R W Gibson. Resolved on the motion of Mr H Holme, seconded by Mr H Brown, that Capt Wingate be formally appointed Hon Secy and Treas of the Fell Pony Society.

Fell Pony Society

Names of Officers and Members of the Committee Elected Oct 10th 1922.

President. Lord Lonsdale.

Vice Presidents. E de V Irving, Esqu.

& G Norris Midwood.

Committee – Mr E de V Irving (Chairman).

Representatives of National Pony Society – 1 G Norris Midwood. 2 Dr R W Gibson.

Representatives of Agricultural Societies –

Hesket Newmarket – 3 Mr A Lawson, 4 Mr J Hind.

Keswick – 5 Mr M Bennett, 6 Mr J Bellas.

Shap – 7 Mr E de V Irving, 8 Mr H Holme.

Appleby – 9 Mr J Dargue, 10 Mr James Wills.

Brough – 11 Mr T Bainbridge, 12 Mr R Sayer.

Kirkby Stephen – 13 Mr J G Marston, 14 Mr E Handley.

Middleton in Teesdale – 15 Mr J W Dent, 16 Mr F Watson.

Sedbergh – 17 Major J Upton, 18 Mr Wm Sedgwick.

Co-opted – 19 Mr J Metcalfe, Heltondale; 20 Mr H Brown, High Winder; 21 Mr H Watson, Uldale; 22 Mr Roy B Charlton, Hexham; 23 Major H M McKenzie, Newton Rigg; 24 Mr W J Wharton, Eamont Lodge, Penrith; 25 Mr John Relph, Turnbank, Shap.

Capt Wingate, Askham, Hon Sec & Treas.

---

28 Nov 1922 (Tuesday), Crown Hotel, Penrith

Proposed by Mr Charlton and seconded by the Chairman that local inspectors should be appointed to inspect all animals eligible for registration and to encourage Fell Pony owners to have their ponies registered. This was carried unanimously.

It was further proposed by Mr Charlton and seconded by Mr Hind that all Stallions for registration should be passed by at least 2 members of the committee. This was carried.

27 March 1923, Crown Hotel, Penrith

It was agreed that a pony already registered as a Fell Pony should not be transferred to the Dales Section nor shall a registered Dales Pony be eligible for the Fell Pony Section and a protest was made against the practice of registering pure bred Fell Ponies in any other section of the Stud Book.

(Agreed by Dales PS, letter from W Patterson 28th April 1924.)

6 Nov 1923 (A meeting of the COUNCIL of the Fell Pony Society), Crown Hotel, Penrith

Mr Charlton proposed that the methods of judging premium stallions should be altered and instead of several shows being held in the various districts one show should be held annually for 1924 at Penrith for the judging of stallion premiums, when ponies should be allocated to various districts by judges, chosen at the general meeting, in consultation with the Hon Secy. Seconded by Mr J Relph and carried.

Mr Charlton proposed a small committee to plan what ponies should go to the London Show.

Letter from JW Dent proposing raising the height of Fell Pony mares to 14 hands. No action to be taken.

24 March 1925 (Council) venue not recorded

It was agreed to ask Penrith Farmers & Kidds Auction to give prizes at the Horse Sale to be held on 24th Sept 1925: Fell ponies 3yrs old and upwards; Fell ponies not exceeding 3 yrs old.

17 Nov 1925 (Council)

To hold a Colt Show on April 27th (1926) in conjunction with the Penrith Agricultural Society Show.

30 November 1926 (Council) at Penrith Farmers' & Kidds Office, Penrith

RB Charlton appointed Secretary, as current Secretary [Capt Wingate] had to resign due to business reasons.

Agreed to accept foal registrations from two registered parents but to leave unaltered the rule about foals from unregistered parents [which had to be inspected before registration; this rule persisted until the stud book closed and only progeny of registered ponies could be accepted].

22 March 1927 ANNUAL GENERAL MEETING, Crown Hotel, Penrith

The Hon Sec explained that it was a considerable time since there had been an Annual General Meeting of the Society; only Council meetings had been held, and the Minutes he read were those of the Council Meeting of 30/11/26. Balance in hand of £19-5s-2d.

Lord Lonsdale to be invited to be Patron, and to elect a President for the year 1927. Lord Henry Cavendish Bentinck, MP, to be asked to be President.

War Office Premiums: repeated award of 5 of £80 each for Fell pony stallions and £10 as prize money for a 2yr old Fell Pony class on Show day. Yearling class to be offered for first time. Stallion licences must be produced before stallions can compete.

Brown 3 year old filly, 2106 Sweet Heather, by Stainmore Fashion out of a brown Fell mare by King of the Mountains; with her prize tickets. Photo from FW Garnett's 'Westmorland Agriculture', 1912

For the season 1912 the Board have allotted £150 for the improvement of Fell ponies in premiums of £20 each to six stallions, and an additional 2/6 for each foal produced, the service fee for such stallions not to exceed 10/- with 2/6 groom's fee—the districts to be travelled being Hesket New Market, Keswick, Shap, Appleby, Kirkby Stephen and Middleton. The premiums were awarded at the various local stallion shows to Lingcropper Again, Highland Fashion, Dreadnought, Dalesman, Blooming Heather II., and Mountain Ranger, to serve respectively in the districts named.

In March, 1909, 33 Fell ponies were sold off the fell with the other stock at Low Roughill, Bampton, when stinted mares 4-8 years old brought 10 to 16 guineas, colts and fillies rising three years old 8 to 11½ guineas, two year olds 7 to 8 guineas, foals 5 to 8 guineas, and a three-year-old stallion 22½ guineas.

The mares get nothing but what they can pull for themselves all winter on the fells and commons, and their poverty causes many of them to slip their foals—their previous season's foal running with them all the time.

Remarks by FW Garnett on the keeping of Fell ponies in 1912 and the allocation of Board of Agriculture premiums for stallions. From Garnett's 'Westmorland Agriculture', 1912

DALES AND FELL PONIES.

Handy Horses for the High Lands.

An article, with the above headings, and illustrated with a photograph of the dales pony stallion, Linnel Comet, appeared in the special Royal Show number of the "North British Agriculturist." The writer says:—

For the Royal Agricultural Society to hold its annual exhibition anywhere in the four northern counties of England—Northumberland, Durham, Cumberland, and Westmorland—without providing a classification for dales and fell ponies, would show a deplorable disregard of the merits of a branch of the equine race that has played, and still plays, an important part in the economics of farming in the high-lying dales and fells of those counties. In the land of heather and bent, of moor and common, these ponies are bred and reared, and, despite competition by heavier breeds of horses, and also despite encouragement held out in the past for the breeding of cross-breds of the "vanner" and "gunner" type, they have remained true to type, and have in their veins real native pony blood.

One speaks of the two breeds together, for really in their foundation and inter-breeding there is not very much difference between them. This is not to deny that the breeders of fell ponies do not see eye to eye with breeders of dales ponies, and vice versa, but, broadly speaking, the question of height is the determining factor, dales ponies being larger ponies of the fell type.

NATIVE TO THE MOORLAND.

Both breeds are native to the mountain and moorland district which has its backbone in the northern section of the Pennines. On the Northumberland, or eastern side, the dales pony is bred; in the strict which has Middleton-in-Teesdale (Durham) for its centre, both the larger and smaller types are found; and, coming over the Pass of Stainmore to the western side of the mountains, the fell pony is met with. This breed is also found on the lakeland fells, with Keswick and Wigton centres, and in the Swaledale and Sedbergh areas of Yorkshire.

The common foundation of the breeds is traced to the hardy "Galloway," which a hundred years and more ago occupied the whole of the Border district, including the south of Scotland. A large part of this was "debateable" land" at the time when border raids were common, and the hardy Galloway was of service both in peace and war. Fleet of foot and strong and sturdy, was the type of animal adapted for border raiding, and it is from such foundations that present-day dales and fell ponies are descended.

Article reproduced in the Penrith Herald from the 'North British Agriculturist', on the nature of local ponies, July 1923.

Photos, Charlton Collection

DRIVEN FROM THE LOWLANDS.

The enclosure of commons and the greater development of agriculture during the nineteenth century meant that the dales and fell ponies were driven from the lowlands, being succeeded by the heavier and more powerful Clydesdale, which, of course, was more adapted to the requirements of arable farms, and, except where a breeder was very keen about maintaining pony type, there was a tendency for the breeds to degenerate and for crossing for the production of a general utility type of animal suitable for sale to dealers or for coaching work. Here and there, however the ideal was not sacrificed, and within the past dozen years or so there has been a great revival in the breeding of pure ponies, this being due to three co-related causes, viz., the formation of breed societies, a steady and improving commercial demand, and the Government scheme of live stock improvement. Especially valuable have been the Ministry of Agriculture premiums for approved stallions and if only all expenditure on the part of that Government department was productive of so much good, what a different tale British agriculture would have to tell

BEING BRED WITH MORE CARE.

Whereas previously, especially in the fell areas, mares, two-year-olds and yearlings, wandered at will over the commons, and fully half were served "loose-headed" by stallions, many of which were not possessed of any special merit, far more care is now exercised, breeders bear in mind questions of type, and only the best of colts are reared as stallions. The greatest care is taken in the award of the premiums, five of which are allocated to the fell pony areas and about a similar number to the dales pony districts, and practically all the stallions travelling with premiums this year are little equine Sandows. That breeding this class of animal is rather more a paying proposition than was at one time the case is conclusively proved by the good demand which has prevailed even during the slump which for two or three years has been the chief feature of the horse trade, and also by the fact that there has been very little, if any, falling off in the number of mares mated. Droves of ponies are sent, fresh from the open common, to Brough Hill, the most famous of the old North of England horse fairs, and last September the trade for them was exceptionally keen when compared with that for heavier horses. Special sales of both dales and fell ponies are now held at various centres.

THE INTER-BREED COMPLICATION.

In addition to having a common foundation, a certain amount of inter-breeding takes place between dales and fell ponies, and, although each breed has a Society catering for its interests, and although each has a separate section in the Stud Book of the National Pony Society, it is not an uncommon thing for a really purebred animal of one breed to be shown as of the other breed. In fact, Mr. Roy Charlton's mare, Robinson's Gypsy, which is of dales pony height, won the Lord Arthur Cecil Memorial Cup at the London Pony Show, being entered as a dales pony, although she was bred in the fell pony district from a fell mare and by a fell stallion, Glengarry. At the same show Lord Lonsdale showed in his first prize fell group a stallion which has a full brother entered in the Stud Book as a dales stallion, while Linnel Heather, bred from dales parents, has held a fell pony premium. But whether dales or fell, these mountain and moorland ponies are a credit to their native districts, and are worthy of inspection by all lovers of Britain's native pony breeds.

PENRITH HERALD JULY 1923

3775 Robinson's Gipsy, who won the Lord Arthur Cecil Memorial Cup at the London Pony Show as a Dales pony. She was by the stallion Glengarry (who was dual registered, 640 Fell and 1019 Dales) out of a Fell pony mare, 2218 Queen of Hearts. Photo, Charlton Collection

SPLENDID STALLIONS

OLDEST STALLION LINES

and their descendants

Stallions of the late 19th and early 20th centuries who are represented in every pedigree by 2018 include:

- Comet -> -> Comet II -> Teesdale Comet (Dales 904) -> Weardale Hero 607 -> Heltondale Victor 938 -> Bob Silvertail 1867 -> Storm Boy 2288;
- Blooming Heather 325;
- Mighty Atom 382 (see *Magnificent Mares*, 2249 Flora III);
- Dalesman 572;
- British Boy 574;
- Little John 599;
- Mountain Ranger 598 -> Hardendale Model 1683;
- Black Jock II 2321 -> Master John 2883.

I have included their photographs if I have found them, but I have nothing for Mighty Atom, British Boy or Little John.

Comet II (Young Comet) - brown

Comet II was bred by William Hully of Bousfield, near Orton. His exact foaling date is uncertain but he was said to be sired by Trotting Comet, a Welsh cob stallion foaled in 1851, registered as a Hackney (1411 HHSB) [Fitzgerald, *Dales Ponies*].

However, the naming of the subsequent "Comets" is hazy, and the names Comet or Young Comet in Fell pedigrees may refer to one horse or two, or possibly more. For instance, a stallion called Total Eclipse 981 foaled in 1917 was registered as sired by Comet (15 hands, brown) who was by Young Comet, (brown, bred by William Hully of the Bousfield stud). The original Trotting Comet 1411 was also known as Comet Talbot because he was bred by Ellis Thomas of the Talbot Hotel in Tregaron, and probably this helped to distinguish him from *his* sire who was also named Trotting Comet (834 HHSB). This line traces back through Flyer and Black Jack to a horse called Cauliflower.

Comet Talbot's owner Dafydd Evans sent him to Westmorland to compete in trotting races, and there he stayed, to sire many "Comet" ponies out of the local stock.

A "Comet" is recorded as the sire of several Fell ponies foaled in the Westmorland Dales between 1897 and 1914. If it is the same horse, he is unlikely to have been foaled before ~1884 (ie, 30 years before). Furthermore, although these stallions were long-lived, a time scale of more than 60 years for two pony generations would be extreme, so going by those progeny dates Comet II was probably a grandson, rather than a son, of the 1851-foaled Comet Talbot. His dam was a galloway mare, either a Fell or Dales.

As a grandson of Comet Talbot, Comet II would have been at least three-quarters local stock, and no more than a quarter Welsh / Hackney. He is described in several pedigrees as brown (probably dark bay) and standing 14.3 or 15 hands. The original of this photograph of him was shown to the FPS Council in 2013 by Bill Potter. It was a large photograph, some 12 inches wide, which hung in the farmhouse at Bousfield.

Paul Metcalfe described the portrait as "a rough looking, common headed cob; you would never think, to look at him, the speed he must have had." There are pencil marks on the photograph outlining the groom's clothing and the horse's legs, which had faded. He may have had ermine marks on his hind socks, which are sometimes seen in Dales ponies today; or the marks may only be part of the pencilling - however, the horse is not, as wrongly asserted in the American magazine *Equus* in 2016, wearing any kind of action enhancing training boots.

The Bousfield stud bred Hackneys, trotting galloway types, Dales, and Fells, some of which won local show classes in Westmorland in the early 1900s.

RB Charlton observed in his 1952 book that Comet's descendants inherited his energy, soundness and stamina. Given that the "Comets" could also be inclined to favour speed over common sense - one killed itself by running away and colliding head-on with a wagon in Orton main street - it is reassuring that Mr Charlton also remarked that "the native [Fell] stock has had the good fortune to keep remarkably free from other outside blood."

Descendants of Comet

A grand-daughter of Comet: 1947 Merry Maid II, dark bay, by Merry John out of 1834 Mountain Maid who was by Comet. 1st prize winner at Kirkby Stephen in 1910 (Polo and Riding Pony Society class for Fell Pony Mares). Photo, Frank W Garnett, Westmorland Agriculture, 1911.

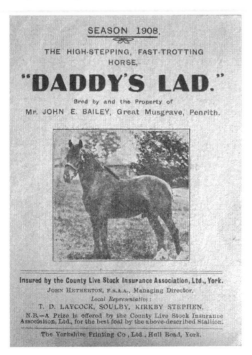

One of Comet's sons, a fast trotter named Daddy's Lad, was at stud at Great Musgrave near Kirkby Stephen for the season 1908, and later was exported to Argentina. Stud card courtesy of the Charlton family archive.

Weardale Hero 607 f.1902 - brown (Comet line)

Weardale Hero 607, f. 1902, by the grey Dales Teesdale Comet 904 out of Nina by Blooming Heather 325. Premium Stallion for the season 1916. Owned by Mr Tom Ireland. Photo from the 1916 Fell Pony Society Report, courtesy of Sharron Gibson Metcalfe.

Weardale Hero was not only a Comet grandson; he was one of several influential stallions whose dam traced to Blooming Heather 325.

In 1916 Weardale Hero served 91 mares in the Shap District, and in 1917, 76 mares, who produced 40 live foals; 22 bay, 11 black, 5 brown and one each grey and chestnut. His foaling percentage of 52.7% was the highest out of the 5 premium stallions that year. In 1918 he served 94 mares. He is another of the premium stallions of this era who are represented in every registered pony today.

There are many other early stallions who are not covered here and whose influence is believed lost: for instance Brough Hill 159 and Eden Grove 160, bred at Widdy Bank in County Durham, whose owners the Lords Cecil lived in Kent; The Mikado 200, f 1889, a broken-coloured horse with an extended pedigree claiming to trace back to Old Grey Shales, but whose owner moved from Appleby to Essex; Merry Hero 327 whose owner lived in Argyllshire; Lothian Prince who won the Premium for Keswick in 1912 but "was not registered by the Polo Society, he being by 'Royal Lothian' (9661 Clydesdale) and therefore not eligible".

Some of these lost bloodlines may possibly have been recaptured through Inspected Stock of the 1950s, but we have no records to show whether that is true or not.

Heltondale Victor 938, f. 1915 - black (Comet line)

Victor was by Weardale Hero 607 out of 1684 Rose, whose dam was by Blooming Heather 325. He was bred by John Jackson, Annie Garth, Martindale, and later owned and shown by John Metcalfe, Dale Foot, Bampton. In 1922 he was a Premium stallion for Shap District and served 100 mares that year. Victor was unusual in having a poem printed on some versions of his card (possibly adapted from one about the Welsh Cob stallion Young King Jack, in 1897):

> Here comes Heltondale Victor,
> We know him by his walk.
> This is the horse that goes so well
> And makes the people talk.
> Look at his head, his neck, his eyes,
> Mark well his shape and size;
> Superior action he displays,
> Amazing strength likewise.

"When the Metcalfes left Dalefoot they sold the herd to Mr Noble as Grandad wanted the horses to stay hefted on Heltondale fell rather than bringing them over to Littlewater and Bampton Common." (Sharron Gibson Metcalfe)

FELL PONY COMMITTEE.

If any particulars are desired as to the service of Fell Pony Mares by this War Office Premium Fell Pony Stallion, application should be made to the District Representatives of the Committee :—

APPLEBY.

Mr. J. Wills, Nether Hoff.

Mr. J. Dargue, Dufton.

Dr. R. W. Gibson, Orton.

or to

Mr. A. L. KIDD,
Hon. Secy.,
St. Andrew's Churchyard,
Penrith.

REED'S LTD., PENRITH.

1924.

PREMIUM
FELL PONY STALLION

"HELTONDALE VICTOR"
No. 938.

The property of

Mr. J. METCALFE,
Dale Foot,
Bampton,
Penrith.

SEASON 1924.

WAR OFFICE
PREMIUM FELL PONY STALLION

District C. - Appleby.

"HELTONDALE VICTOR,"
No. 938.

The Property of Mr. J. METCALFE, Dale Foot, Bampton, Penrith, having been awarded the £60 Premium, will serve the Fell Pony Mares in the Appleby District at 15/- each, with 2/6 Groom's Fee, due at time of service.

ROUTE :

Commencing May 12th, 1924.

Monday :

Colby, Appleby, Murton, Hilton, Dufton to Long Marton, over night.

Tuesday :

Knock, Gullum, Milburn to Blencarn, over night.

Wednesday :

Newbiggin, Kirkbythore, Bolton and Kings Meaburn.

Thursday :

Sleagill, Morland, Newby and Maulds Meaburn.

Friday :

Reagill, Oddendale, Crosby Ravensworth.

Saturday :

Home over weekend.

"Heltondale Victor" 938, black, foaled 1915, 13.2 h.h. ; sire "Weardale Hero" 607, dam "Rose" by "Mountain Boy," 2nd dam "Bess" by "Blooming Heather," 3rd dam "Brown Bess" by "Mountain Hero."

He will travel with the Ministry of Agriculture Certificate of Soundness, which is open to inspection.

Mr. Metcalfe will not be answerable for any loss or damage through the trying or serving of Mares, but every care will be taken.

All Mares tried by this horse and served by another, or sold, exchanged, or given away will be charged full price.

Victor's card in 1924 was donated by Sharron Gibson Metcalfe in 2021. Interestingly, the extended pedigree shows the dam line, not the sire line: Sire Weardale Hero 607, Dam Rose by Mountain Boy, 2nd Dam Bess by Blooming Heather, 3rd Dam Brown Bess by Mountain Hero.

Bob Silvertail 1867 f.1923 - black (Comet line)

Bob Silvertail 1867 was bred in 1923 by Robert Dunning of Barugh, Tebay, and sired by Heltondale Victor 938 out of John Dunning's homebred mare 2545 Queen of the Dales by Merry John. Bob Silvertail was known for the grey in his tail and for an unusually difficult temperament. By 1927 he belonged to Messrs Wharton of Tebay, and he was sold in the reduction sale reported below. M Thompson, Garnet Bridge, Kendal, owned him in the 1930s.

"FIFTY YEARS A WESTMORLAND PONY BREEDER

"Mr Tom Wharton, Cocklake Farm, Tebay, whose sale of pure-bred Fell ponies took place on Saturday week, as was reported in Tuesday's "Observer," has for nearly fifty years been connected with Fell Pony breeding. He and his brother, Mr W J Wharton, Eamont Lodge, Penrith, who is a most enthusiastic Fell Pony fancier, have figured prominently as breeders and exhibitors during the past few years, and to their credit they have always shown their stock "in the rough". ...

"Some of the ponies which Messrs Wharton sold on Saturday are descended from a young dark grey mare, which Mr Tom Wharton bought from the late Mr Thomas Sanderson, Red Gill, nearly fifty years ago, and that strain at Cocklake has been named Lucy's strain. Twenty years ago Mr T Wharton brought into Westmorland Heather's Model, one of the many good sons of old Blooming Heather, and bred by the late Mr William Dalton, Snowhope Close, Stanhope, Durham. Heather's Model figures in the pedigree of many of the best Fell Ponies of today, ... (eg) Tailbert Short Tail, which was cup winner at the National Pony Show of 1926, and also winner of the Frank Garnett Perpetual Challenge Cup at the Penrith Show, an award which is the blue riband of the Fell Pony Show world.

"... Messrs Wharton are not absolutely retiring from the Fell pony ranks, and one of the ponies they have reserved is a yearling entire colt [Woodend Moonlight 1550 by Black Jock 1122 x 5671 Wood-end Velvet] which won its class at both the Penrith and Westmorland Shows, being reserve for the Garnett Cup ... At the sale there was a fair demand. Mares made to £21.10s to Mr Roy Charlton, two-year-old fillies to £15, two-year-old geldings £11, and a four-year-old stallion (Bob Silver Tail) £19 10s." Penrith Observer - Tuesday 04 October 1927

In the ownership of the Wharton family (Eamont Bridge and Tebay) Bob Silvertail sired the very influential stallion Storm Boy 2288 f.1933, and 5648 Linnel Wanda f.1927 (see p114), one of several mares bought by His Majesty King George V for his own use and as the foundation of the Balmoral Stud.

Bob Silvertail was used for a time in Kentmere Quarries in the hope that the hard work might quieten him down. Whether it did or not, the quarry foreman's young daughter is said to have got on well with him and could do anything with him.

Park House Victor 2850 f. 1937 - black (Comet line).

Park House Victor 2850 was by Bob Silvertail 1867 out of Mable, who was by Blooming Heather III 670. He was bred by JJ Taylor, Longmire Yeat, Troutbeck, Windermere.

This photograph included in the FPS Report for 1950 is unflattering, but Victor must have been popular because he was awarded the Premium for the FPS Enclosure for three successive years: at High Arnside in 1951, and in 1952 and '53 at Crag House, Windermere. He was the sire of Miss Crossland's well known stallion Packway Royal 3276 (18 progeny including Heltondales) and his influence was carried by some of Henry Harrison's best known Sleddale mares, including the Dainty, Rosette and Beauty lines.

" PARK HOUSE VICTOR," Premium Stallion.

Photo from the FPS Report of 1950, in the FPS papers in the Cumbria Archive Centre, Kendal.

The Enclosure records for Windermere in 1952 showing which mares ran with Victor.

Storm Boy 2288 f. 1933 - black (Comet line)

"Storm Boy"

Photo from the FPS Report of 1950, in the FPS papers in the Cumbria Archive Centre, Kendal.

Storm Boy 2288 was bred by W Wharton & Son, Eamont Lodge, Eamont Bridge, Penrith, by Bob Silvertail 1867 out of 6551 Woodend Lady Atkinson.

For the War Office premiums for Fell ponies—a total sum of £300 was offered—there were six entries for five premiums. Five of the six had held premiums previously, a new one being Storm Boy, a six-year-old by Mountain Jester *[sic; this does not agree with the FPS registration, and Jester is not recorded as a sire of ponies bred by the Whartons]* owned by Mr J Baxter, Guardhouse, Threlkeld. This pony was awarded the Shap district premium... *Penrith Observer, Tuesday 02 May 1939*

Storm Boy was awarded premiums in subsequent years including the Travelling premium for 1951, so he was the sire of many well known ponies and of champion stallions such as Mountain Model 2884 and Blakebeck Boy 2842 (following pages).

Mr AW Morland (Lunesdale Stud) also has copies of these photographs of Storm Boy and his son Mountain Model. About Storm Boy, he commented, "If he had a fault, he was rather thick in his lower neck but the rest of him was very correct. He had a nice head, a well laid shoulder, a short back, and good legs and feet."

Joe Baxter's grand-daughter Eileen and her friends used to go and "laik on" with Joe's home-bred ponies at Guardhouse and have them more than half broken before they went for sale. "Storm Boy was a reet black 'un. He was my favourite. But if Granda saw the ponies looking to us for treats he'd say, 'Now you haven't been taking my corn for them, have you!'" Eileen looked after Storm Boy, at the end of his life, at her mother's house at Towcett, Shap.

Mountain Model 2884 f. 1948 - black (Comet line)

Photo from the FPS Report of 1950, in the FPS papers in the Cumbria Archive Centre, Kendal.

Mountain Model 2884 won two first prizes as a foal at Hesket-New-Market Show in 1948. He was by Storm Boy 2288, out of 8241 Mountain Gypsy by Mountain Jester 1409.

Owned and bred by William Winder, Low Fellside, Caldbeck, Model was champion stallion at the Stallion and Colt show in 1951, 1952 and 1953, standing each season in the Berrier Enclosure.

No Publicity is Bad Publicity...

Penrith Observer, Tuesday 15 March 1927

FELL PONIES IN LONDON. SUCCESS OF LOCAL EXHIBITS.

At the London Pony Show the "cave man" ponies from the Dales, Fells, and the Highlands, presented an attractive display. Mr J Bellas, Keswick, won in stallions, with a brown Fell pony, Moor Lad, bred by Mr J W Dalton...

Blakebeck Boy 2842 f. 1948 -black (Comet line)

Harry Wales (Lownthwaite ponies) with Blakebeck Boy 2842 at the Stallion Show in 1956 when he was chosen as Premium Stallion for the Berrier Enclosure. Photograph from the FPS Archive, taken by Joseph Hardman.

By Storm Boy 2288 out of 8959 Blakebeck Jess, by Woodend Banker 1866. I remember David Trotter saying of this stallion, "He wasn't very big, but what a thick 'oss all the same." FPS President Christine Morton recalls: "Blakebeck Boy was sold to Reuben Tunstall and went into the Dales Stud book, as noted in Iona Fitzgerald's book Dales Ponies. We still use those bit converters [on the headcollar], stallion bit and plough line for serving mares with."

1956

Fell winner, Mr P. A. Lawson's BLAKEBECK BOY, black stallion, 17 years, by Storm Boy out of Blakebeck Jess, bred by W. and A. Mandale, Troutbeck, Penrith. He was also reserve in the Merlin Cup Mountain and Moorland championship to Criban Victor

The Stallion Premium Scheme

In the Report for 1912 of the Fell Pony Committee, a Fell Pony breeding scheme had been approved by the Board of Agriculture, by which £150 was to be used to provide premiums for travelling stallions for each of the Districts: A, Hesket-New-Market; B, Keswick; C, Shap; D, Appleby; E, Kirkby Stephen; and F, Middleton in Teesdale, each of which had its own show to choose its Premium stallion. The judges for each show were nominated by a committee local to the area.

£20 was paid to the owner of each chosen Premium stallion for that season, with 2 shillings and 6 pence for each foal produced the following year; the owner was allowed to charge for the stallion's services, but the fee must not be more than 10 shillings plus a groom's fee of 2 shillings and 6 pence.

Fell Pony Committee Secretary Frank Garnett estimated that in 1912 the 6 Premium travelling stallions had averaged 36 services apiece, almost 60% of services getting live foals. (By 1917 the average number of services by the 5 Premium stallions had increased to 61, but foaling percentage in 1918 was 43%.)

Garnett knew of 30 working Fell stallions in 1912 and so he estimated there were at least 1,080 mares in the area (ie, 30 x average of 36 services), although "the District covered by the Committee does not cover the entire Fell Pony Country." In 1914 he also wrote that:

>"of the five Premium stallions all without exception are descended on their sire or dam's side from Blooming Heather 325 and the time is fast approaching when the question of introducing fresh blood must be faced. It must be borne in mind that the Highland pony, ie the original Galloway, and our own, now called the Fell pony, are of one and the same foundation breed, and the interchange of stallions between the two districts in which they are bred has been continuous from time out of mind. In seeking new blood again, the selection of the very best blacks and browns of these ponies would seem to be indicated."

"A visit to the Fell mares, near to Angle Tarn Pykes." No date. Photo, Charlton Collection

Blooming Heather 325 f. 1880 - black

Blooming Heather 325, f. about 1880, by Little John out of Polly.
Photo, the Beamish People's Collection.

Blooming Heather 325 was by Little John out of Polly; both sire and dam were brown, and Blooming Heather was black, maturing at 13.2 hands. His sire Little John, an unbeaten trotting pony, traced back through Merry John / Merry Driver (1045 Hackney) / Shales the Original / Blaze, and thence to Flying Childers. Flying Childers, famous as an early Thoroughbred sire, was by the Darley Arabian out of Betty Leedes, a racing mare of Galloway, Irish Hobby and Barb breeding.

Blooming Heather was bred about 1880 by Mr R Tunstall of Stainmore, and later owned by Mr John Gibson of Widdy Bank in Teesdale. Unsurprisingly, given his ancestry, he too was a very fast trotter, and as a sire he passed on his speed: one of his sons needed a big horse to gallop to keep up with him. Like other popular pony stallions of his era, he was used on both Fell and Dales mares. He was still serving Fell mares in 1907.

RB Charlton [in his book *A Lifetime With Ponies*] recalls the evening when he walked up from the Langdon Beck Hotel to Widdy Bank to see the famous stallion, arriving after dark to Mr Gibson's surprise.

> "[The pony] was in a miserable old stable where the little horse was standing up to his knees in a bracken bed ... Blooming Heather and his surroundings disappointed me dreadfully. He was a common looking pony, with not a neat head, but he appeared to be standing on good sound legs and feet ... Teesdale is famous for three things only. A bit of Steel Shipbuilding, High Force and 'Blooming Heather'."

Descendants of Blooming Heather

Blooming Heather II 566 f. 1902- dark brown (Blooming Heather line)

Joe Relph with Blooming Heather II 566, f. 1902, brown, by Blooming Heather 325 out of Queen of the Dales. Bred by Thomas Fishwick of Rosgill near Shap. Photo, Charlton Collection

It is always interesting to study photographs of ponies and the way they are presented for a show or for the camera. In the early 20th C it was the fashion to stand ponies "stretched" to cover as much ground as possible. The photographers have been careful to stand at right angles to the pony, rather than three-quarters on, which would distort the image and make the head and neck seem disproportionately large.

Black Blooming Heather 674 (next page) looks as though he was photographed ready for travelling, with the stallion man's overnight belongings strapped to his surcingle. Stallion tack was usual for control, and was quite often of white leather. Notice how far back the surcingle is fitted, not only in these photos but in those on previous pages. It was said in those days that a horse who "throws his girth into his elbows" should be relegated to harness work because he would have a steep shoulder and a short stride and be a choppy ride; so for advertising purposes the surcingle was usually strategically placed closer to the visual halfway point of the pony's body, rather than in the "girth groove". This - particularly with white harness - was meant to show off well laid shoulders and shortness of back.

Heather Blossom 647 (next page) is notable from a historical perspective as he was one of the few early stallions recorded as owned and bred by a woman - the first being Lord Briton 249 f.1898, bred by Miss Martha Wearmouth, Ossett, Yorkshire. Mrs Davies who bred Heather Blossom lived in Westmorland, between Orton and Tebay, in the early part of the 20th C; her farmhouse, Daniel Hill, was derelict before I moved to Greenholme in 1983. It stood near the northbound Westmorland Services on the M6 motorway. It finally collapsed only a few years ago.

Black Blooming Heather II 674 f. 1908. (Blooming Heather line)

Black Blooming Heather 674 f 1908. By Blooming Heather 325 out of a black Fell mare by Comet.
Bred by John Cragg of Dent (which was then in Yorkshire), and later transferred to the Dales stud
book. Photo: Charlton collection.

Heather Blossom 647, f 1917 - black (Blooming Heather line)

Heather Blossom 647, f 1917, black, by Heather's Model 381 by Blooming Heather 325, out of 2271
Mountain Lass III by Sir George. Bred by Mrs Agnes H Davies, Daniel Hill, Orton.
Photo: Charlton collection.

Dalesman 572 f. 1902 - dark brown

Dalesman 572 at the age of 21 winning first prize for Dales Pony Stallions at the Royal Show at Newcastle in 1923. Photo: FPS Archives

Foaled in 1902, Dalesman was bred by Mr R Bousfield, Whygill Head, Great Asby. He was sired by Yorkshire Fashion out of Doll, a brown 13.2 mare, and was a 1st prize winner at Brough as a foal and at Shap as a yearling.

In the ownership of Mr John Relph, Turn Bank, Maulds Meaburn, he travelled the Appleby District for 1912 and served 50 mares. In 1915 he served 52 mares and produced 36 foals; in 1918 he travelled Shap District. After 1920 he was not allowed to compete for the Ministry Premiums in the Appleby or Shap Districts "in consequence of the number of years [he has] travelled those Districts." He was still serving Fell mares in 1923 although (as in the show photo above) he was probably better known in Dales classes.

He was a highly popular sire throughout his life and was honoured with an obituary (next page) in the Penrith Herald in 1934, which was probably written by RB Charlton of Hexham.

"By the death of Dalesman, the greatest Fell or Dales pony stallion of the past quarter century, North Country pony breeding has lost its Dunure Footprint."

Dunure Footprint 15203 CHSB, to whom Dalesman was compared in the obituary, was a famous bay Clydesdale stallion foaled 1909, and a winner of many championships.
His left foreleg was black to the shoulder, with a patch of white on the forearm.

14-THE HERALD.

By the death of Dalesman, the greatest Fell or Dales pony stallion of the past quarter century, North country pony breeding has lost its Dunure Footprint.

Dalesman, in the ownership of Mr. John Relph, Turnbank, Newby, reached the age of 32 years. It won more Government premiums than any other pony; its stock have been supreme in the showyard throughout many equine generations.

When the Royal Show was held at Newcastle in 1923, the following sentences occurred in the "Herald's" report of the Dales pony classes: "It was a tribute to the stamina and excellence of that famous old stallion Dalesman that it should again head the aged stallion class at the Royal Show for its owner, Mr. John Relph, Turn Bank, Newby, near Penrith. Now 21 years old, and bred by the late Mr. R. Bousfield, Whygill Head, Little Asby, Dalesman is showing signs of age but is still remarkably fresh."

These words were written eleven years ago: Dalesman was an old horse then, but by no means at the end of his career, as subsequent events proved.

Dalesman—was he a Fell pony or a Dales? He was bred in the Fell country, but, because of his size, was registered in the Dales section of the National Pony Society stud book. He was just as valuable to the one breed as to the other; it was common at one time to have his progeny winning for both Fell and Dales ponies at the same show! But, in size, he was a Dales, standing 14-2 h.h., and sired by Yorkshire Fashion.

Dalesman combined real pony character with the weight of a cob. His abundant vitality was inherited by his offspring, as, for instance, his grand-daughter, Robinson's Gypsy. She was shown at the same Royal Show at Newcastle, and displayed that " vim " which was so characteristic of her. That good judge of horse flesh, Sir Merick Burrell, rode her that day; and to a friend he expressed his delight at the splendid ride, commenting that he was surprised how easily the mare carried weight. Robinson's Gypsy won the pony riding class that day; six years later she was the winner at the Royal at Harrogate; and she was also twice champion brood mare of all mountain and moorland breeds at the National Pony Show in London, these successes being in 1922 and 1923.

Now, to mention two daughters of Dalesman—Linnel Flirt and Linnel Fancy, both bred by Mr. Henry Holme at Thrimby and later the property of Mr. R. B. Charlton, the hon. secretary of the Fell Pony Society.

Following Robinson's Gypsy's London Show successes in 1922 and 1923 (she was Dalesman's grand-daughter, be it remembered), Linnel Flirt stood in the same position in 1924. Her daughter, Linnel Fluff, won the Sir Arthur Cecil Memorial Cup in London in 1932, and is now the property of H.M. The King.

Linnel Fancy, the other daughter of Dales-

man, also became a first prize winner in London, and, through her alone, Dalesman has been the fore-elder of such ponies as Linnel Brown Boy, Linnel Boy, Linnel Darkie, Linnel Snip, Linnel Gallant Boy, and lots more, including at least four now in Spain.

Again, Linnel Lingeropper, champion stallion at London in 1931 and 1932 and winner of H.M. The King's premium at Penrith last April, was Dalesman's great-grandson.

This is dealing with Dalesman's progeny in one line only. What a task it would be to trace even all the notable ponies! Bess of Hardendale, a Fell pony mare of true type and one of Dalesman's daughters, is at the head ofanother family.

So far one has mentioned only Fell ponies, and these only in a limited circle. Dalesman had equally as many Dales pony descendants. Ouston Model, bred by the late Mr. Samuel Walton, Ouston, Whitfield, was a son of Dalesman. Ouston Model was a noted pony, and was eventually exported to Spain by Mr. Joseph Johnson, Crook. Another Dales son of Dalesman was exported along with five Fell mares to set up a stud in Michigan, U.S.A.

One has perhaps written enough; suffice to say that as long as Fell and Dales ponies have their supporters, the name of Dalesman will be recalled. This pony travelled from the inception of the Board of Agriculture grants; probably more than any other pony, Dalesman perpetuated true pony character in Cumberland, Westmorland, Durham and Northumberland.

Dalesman, as already mentioned, belonged to the veteran Mr. John Relph, Turnbank, and he it was who kept the old pony not only in the days of its supremacy but in its later years. Dalesman was never beaten in the show ring, so Mr. Relph assures us; its last appearance was at the 1923 Royal— when the photograph we reproduce was taken. One may add that when Mr. Relph showed that other noted pony Glengarry in London it was the supreme champion of all the mountain and moorland breeds, winning a fifty guinea trophy presented by " Country Life." On that occasion, Mr. Relph received the cup at the hands of Queen Alexandra, and was accompanied to the Royal box by Mr. H. Holme, of Thrimby.

To those who have kept the Fell pony breed going through difficult times, the passing of Dalesman is a reminder of the good work that was done for the Fell pony breed when the late Mr. Frank Garnett and others founded the Fell Pony Society. It is sad to think that their labours have been so sadly spoiled by the summary withdrawal of the Government grants towards pony breeding, for, without those premiums for stallions, it is clear that Fell and Dales pony breeding will pass out, except it be as a hobby for a few. If it could only be made possible to put a few pure-bred stallions on the road the breed could be saved—but it is a big " If."

Obituary for Dalesman in the Herald, 1934, from the Charlton Collection.

"Dalesman, in the ownership of Mr John Relph, Turnbank, Newby, reached the age of 32 years. It won more Government premiums than any other pony; its stock have been supreme in the showyard through many equine generations.

"When the Royal Show was held at Newcastle in 1923, the following sentences occurred in the "Herald's" report of the Sales pony classes: "It was a tribute to the stamina and excellence of that famous old stallion Dalesman that it should again head the aged stallion class at the Royal Show for its owner, Mr John Relph, Turn Bank, Newby, near Penrith. Now 21 years old, and bred by the late Mr R Bousfield, Whygill Head, Little Asby, Dalesman is showing signs of age but is still remarkably fresh. ...

"Dalesman - was he a Fell pony or a Dales? He was bred in the Fell country, but, because of his size, was registered in the Dales section of the National Pony Society stud book. He was just as valuable to the one breed as to the other; it was common at one time to have his progeny winning for both Fell and Dales ponies at the same show!

"Dalesman combined real pony character with the weight of a cob. His abundant vitality was inherited by his offspring, as, for instance, his grand-daughter, Robinson's Gypsy. She was shown at the same Royal Show at Newcastle, and displayed that "vim" which was so characteristic of her. That good judge of horse flesh, Sir Merrick Burrell, rode her that day; and to a friend he expressed his delight at the splendid ride, commenting that he was surprised how easily the mare carried weight. Robinson's Gypsy won the pony riding class that day; six years later she was the winner at the Royal at Harrogate; and she was also twice champion brood mare of all mountain and moorland breeds at the National Pony Show in London, these successes being in 1922 and 1923.

"Now, to mention two daughters of Dalesman, Linnel Flirt and Linnel Fancy, both bred by Mr Henry Holme at Thrimby, and later the property of Mr R B Charlton, the hon. secretary of the Fell Pony Society.

"Following Robinson's Gypsy's London Show successes in 1922 and 1923 ... Linnel Flirt stood in the same position in 1924. Her daughter, Linnel Fluff, won the Sir Arthur Cecil Memorial Cup in London in 1932, and is now the property of HM The King.

"Linnel Fancy, the other daughter of Dalesman, also became a first prize winner in London, and, through her alone, Dalesman has been the fore-elder of such ponies as Linnel Brown Boy, Linnel Boy, Linnel Darkie, Linnel Snip, Linnel Gallant Boy, and lots more, including at least four now in Spain. ...

"Probably more than any other pony, Dalesman perpetuated true pony character in Cumberland, Westmorland, Durham and Northumberland."

Mountain Ranger 598 f. 1906 - black

Mountain Ranger 598 was bred in 1906 by JW Dent of Stanhope Gate, Middleton-in-Teesdale. He stood 13.3 hands and was by Park End King, a grey, out of Scordale Queen, also grey. Scordale Queen was by Blooming Heather 325 so this line also goes back to him.

A very popular stallion, Mountain Ranger was awarded Premiums to travel several Districts including Middleton, Keswick and Shap. In 1912 Mountain Ranger served 29 mares; in 1916 in the ownership of Mr J Bussey he served 89 and got 41 foals; in 1917, he served 102 mares and got 38 foals.

In the 1922 season, as Premium stallion for Keswick District in the ownership of Mr Joe Baxter of Threlkeld, he served 100 mares; for Shap District in 1923, 60.

In February 1923 he and two mares (4209 Moor Daisy II and 4190 Baggra Yeat Bella) were shown as a Fell pony group at the National Pony Society Show in London and the group was placed 4th.

His famous descendants in the direct male line include Hardendale Model 1683 (one of his last foals, in 1927), Heltondale Prince 3751, Townend Flash II 5278, Tebay Campbellton Victor 6614, Heltondale Black Prince III FP188C and many more.

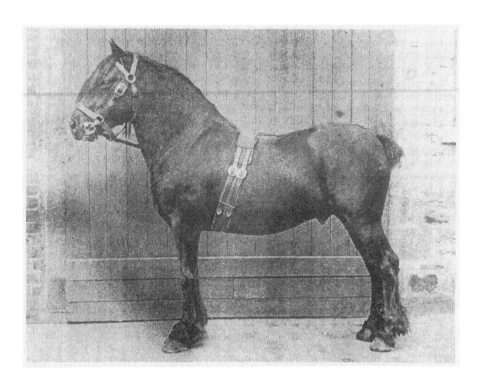

Mountain Ranger, Premium stallion in 1918 for Middleton in Teesdale, a District which he travelled for several seasons. Photo in the FPS Archives.

Mountain Ranger in a trotting sulky, about to set off on his rounds as a travelling stallion in the ownership of Mr J Bussey: the sulky, so named for its single seat, was a less strenuous way for the stallion man to travel, compared to walking beside the horse. Photo from the 1916 Report of the Fell Pony Committee, courtesy of Sharron Gibson Metcalfe.

By contrast to Mr Bussey's style of travelling, when Joe Baxter owned Mountain Ranger in the 1920s he would walk leading the stallion, with his coat strapped to the surcingle together with a "bait-bag" containing oats for the stallion and a day's food for himself, and maybe a few "bare necessities" in the coat pockets for the night's stopover. In the Shap District (see next page) they walked approximately 88 miles each week. Mr Baxter, a short man "as agile as a monkey and very skilled in the work", lived well into his nineties.

Joe Baxter "walking" Master John 2883 (page 66) probably in 1952. Master John was probably the last Fell stallion to hold a Travelling Premium, in 1958, still in the ownership of Joe Baxter. Photo, FPS News Vol V, taken by Peggy Crossland, "at the back o'Skidda", which usually refers to the Uldale fells north of Bassenthwaite.

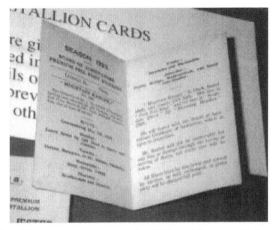

Stud card for Mountain Ranger in the Fell Pony Museum at Dalemain

BOARD OF AGRICULTURE PREMIUM
FELL PONY STALLION

District B. - Shap

"MOUNTAIN RANGER" No. 598

The Property of Mr J Baxter of Threlkeld, having been awarded the £60 Premium, will cover Fell Pony Mares at 15/- each, with 2/6 Groom's Fee, due at time of service.

ROUTE

Commencing May 7th, 1923.

Monday: Leave by Gill Head to Dacre and Askham. *[approx 20 miles]*

Tuesday: Helton, Bampton, to Mr Holme, Thrimby. *[approx 8 miles]*

Wednesday: Shap, Orton, Tebay. *[approx 15 miles]*

Thursday: Bretherdale and District. *[approx 7 miles: includes the Greenholme area so could be very variable as there were several breeders around there]*

Friday: Howtown and Martindale. *[approx 20 miles]*

Saturday: Pooley Bridge, Watermillock, and home over Sunday. *[approx 18 miles]*

"Mountain Ranger" is black, foaled 1906, and stands 13.3 high. His sire is "Park End King" and his dam is "Scoredale Queen" by "Blooming Heather" (325).

He will travel with the Board of Agriculture Certificate of Soundness, which is open to inspection.

Mr Baxter will not be answerable for any loss or damage through the trying or serving of mares, but every care will be taken.

All Mares tried by this horse and served by another, or sold, exchanged, or given away will be charged full price.

Descendants of Mountain Ranger: Hardendale Model 1683 f.1927 - brown

Hardendale Model, shown by Messrs J. Brunskill and Son, Hardendale, the winner of the War Office premium for Fell Pony Stallions.

Hardendale Model 1683, by Mountain Ranger 598 out of 5616 Hardendale Gem (by Heltondale Victor 938). Photo, courtesy of John Brunskill's grandson John Greig, Nelson Farm, Hardendale.

Hardendale Model, owned and bred by John Brunskill and Son, Hardendale Hall, Shap, was a popular stallion in the area in the 1930s. Born in 1927, he was dark brown with a white star and a little white on one fetlock. He measured 13.3hh in 1930.

The Wigton District Agricultural Society, on Tuesday afternoon held their 53rd annual show of Entire Horses ... For the first time for many years a Fell Pony was shown, Mr J. H. Edgar's (Workington), Hardendale Model, sired by Mountain Ranger. He was premium horse in Keswick district last year and expects to attain another premium this year. *Wigton Advertiser - Saturday 22 April 1939*

After a year in the Keswick District in 1938 he held the War Office Premium for stallions (photo, above) for the Shap District in 1939.

FELL PONIES For the War Office premiums for Fell ponies—a total sum of £300 was offered—there were six entries for five premiums. Storm Boy...was awarded the Shap district premium, and the other premiums were allotted as follows: Hardendale Model, owned by Mr. Edgar, Workington, to travel the Keswick area; Fell Model, owned by Mr. Lund, Ravenstonedale, to travel Kirkby Stephen district: Monks Mountain Ranger, owned by Mr. J. W. Dent, Middleton-in-Teesdale, to travel the Middleton-in-Teesdale district; and Coronation Boy, owned by Mr. H. Brunskill, Milburn Grange, Appleby, to travel the Appleby district. *Penrith Observer - Tuesday 02 May 1939*

Hardendale Model is believed to have won a class at the Royal Show when it was held at Blackpool, Lancashire.

Heltondale Romer 2540 f. 1939 - dark brown (Mountain Ranger line)

Heltondale Romer 2540 f. 1939, by Jock of Askham Gate, by Mountain Ranger.
Photo, FPS Report 1950, courtesy of Mr AW Morland.

Heltondale Prince 3751 f. 1951 - dark brown (Mountain Ranger line)

Heltondale Prince 3751 "in his working clothes" during the breeding season. By Heltondale Romer
2540 out of 8185 Blackbird VII. Photo, courtesy of Greta Noble.

Htd Rambler II 4749, F 1965 - brown (Mountain Ranger line)

Heltondale Rambler II by Htd Mountain Prince 4184 (by Htd Prince 3571) x 12939 Htd Rosie with Ted Potter at Greenholme Show. Photo, FPS archive.

Townend Flash II 5278 f. 1969 - black (Mountain Ranger line)

Townend Flash II 5278 with Glenis Wilson. Flash was by Lunesdale Richard 4637 (Htd Sonny Boy 4473 / Htd Star Boy 3854 / Htd Prince 3751) out of 10976 Townend Polly VI (by Master John 2883). Photo, courtesy of Penny Randell.

Tebay Campbellton Victor 6614 f. 1976 - black (Mountain Ranger line)

Victor was bred in 1976 by David Trotter of Tebay, by Lownthwaite Star Dust 5965 (sire line Townend Prince 5188/Lunesdale Richard 4637/Heltondale Sonny Boy 4473/Htd Star Boy 3854/Htd Romer 2540) out of 15877 Tebay Brandy.

His great-grand-dam in the tail female line was an Inspected mare, 12941 Heltondale Mary (I.S.) whose antecedents are unknown. She may have carried a rare or "lost" line or, more probably, one or more of the lines from the popular stallions already mentioned. "Those who really know are no longer around to tell us. Just because an ancestor doesn't appear in pedigrees doesn't mean it isn't behind modern day Fell Ponies. For instance, the ancestor could

Tebay Campbellton Victor 6614, f.1976, at the Stallion Show at Dalemain, shown by Bill Potter.
Photo, Ruth Eastwood

have been behind a pony accepted into the stud book through the Inspection or Grading Up Schemes. These ponies didn't have pedigrees (registered sires and dams) but were found to be of proper type at the time. It is possible, then, that they could represent ancestors that aren't otherwise represented by ponies produced from registered parents. We will never know for sure. ... Tebay Campbellton Victor was behind 53% of foals in the 2005 and 2006 foal crops and his average contribution to the 2017 and 2018 foal crops was 84%." *[comments and data analysis by Jenifer Morrissey, Willowtrail, USA; using software to calculate from FPS Stud Book records how many foals in a given year are descended from a particular pony].*

Victor stood 12.2hh with very abundant mane, tail and feather. He was used for several years each in the Tebay and Heltondale studs. Victor, and ponies got by him, were said to be a good "nick" with Black Prince's stock, such matings usually producing excellent ponies. (Examples later in the book.)

Heltondale Black Prince III f. 1982 - black (Mountain Ranger line)

Prince was bred in 1982 by Sarge Noble, by Hardendale Raven 7055 (sire line Moorhouse Black Prince 6117/Htd Black Prince II 5643/Htd Ranger 4778/Htd Mountain Prince 4184/Htd Prince 3751/Htd Romer 2540).

His dam was 13925 Heltondale Beauty III, by Glenwelt 4546 (Merry John / Master John / Black Jock II) out of 12843 Heltondale Dido who carried the Heltondale Romer line on both her sire's and dam's side. Heltondale Black Prince III was behind 69% of foals in the 2005 and 2006 foal crops and his average contribution to the 2017 and 2018 foal crops (as recorded in the FPS Stud Books) was 93% [Jenifer Morrissey].

Heltondale Black Prince III FP188C, f. 1982, with his breeder Sarge Noble, in May 1988 at Bampton. Photo, Mrs Greta Noble.

Sarge Noble gave Peter Boustead the job of breaking Prince to ride. Peter remembers Prince's enormous bellowing neigh, which startled one of his acquaintances into the remark, "What the hell have you got in that stable, a Charolais bull!" Prince was "up to height" and in later life (in Germany) was measured as over 14hh. The photographs have been scaled and positioned here to approximate the relative sizes of these two stallions. Black Prince III and Victor were extremely influential in the late 20th C, Black Prince III having 232 registered offspring and Victor 176. Both are directly descended in the male line from Mountain Ranger, Prince's tail female line also being from Htd Romer (Mountain Ranger line). Prince was used for several years each in the Heltondale, Greenholme and Murthwaite studs.

The huge popularity of Victor and Prince in the 1980s and '90s made it harder to find unrelated matches in subsequent generations. Each of these stallions will have his own chapter further on.

Glengarry 640 f. 1911- black

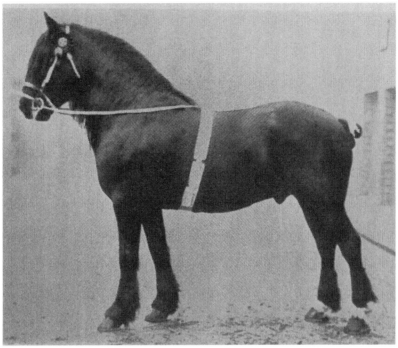

Sired by British Boy 574 out of a grey mare, Fanny, Glengarry 640 was another Premium stallion whose dam was by Blooming Heather 325. Photo, Charlton Collection.

Glengarry was black, and measured 13.1hh at age 3 and a little taller with maturity. He was, like many other stallions of the era, dual-registered as both a Fell and a Dales; in the Dales stud book he was stallion 1019.

Bred by Thomas Glen of Brackenber, Appleby, he travelled in the ownership of John Relph, Turn Bank, Shap, and in the Shap District in 1915 he served 50 mares who produced 25 foals in 1916.

In Appleby District in 1916 he served 66 mares who produced 41 foals in 1917, the highest foaling percentage for a Premium stallion that year. In 1918, he served 49 mares.

Interior page of the stud card for "the double champion Pony Stallion Glengarry" for 1916, courtesy of Mrs Beatrice Bainbridge

Agricultural Society's District, and in 1915 he won the £40 Premium, offered by the Board of Agriculture, to travel the Shap Society's District.

At the National Pony Show held in the Agricultural Hall. Islington, on March 2nd, 1916, he took First Prize of £12 as one of a group of three, and was at the same time awarded the Champion Trophy, value 50 guineas, in an entry of forty-eight exhibits, as the best pony in the hall (a marvellous feat.)

He will travel with the Board of Agriculture Certificate of soundness, which is open for inspection by all comers.

The owner will not be responsible for any loss or damage through the trying or serving of any mare, or to persons in charge, but every care will be taken.

All mares once tried by this horse, sold, exchanged, or given away, will be charged full season's price. No allowance for mares that lose their foals.

In the event of this horse not being fit for service, the owner reserves the right to substitute another in his place, on same conditions.

For Terms, apply to Owner or Groom in charge.

Postal Address: TURN BANK, SHAP, S.O.
Telegrams: MORLAND, PENRITH.

The Glengarry line

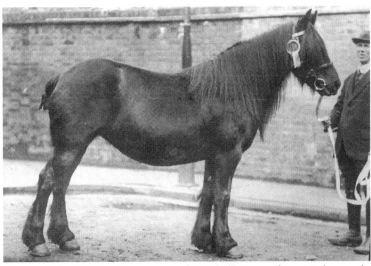

3775 Robinson's Gipsy f.1917, by Glengarry out of 2218 (Fell) Queen of Hearts, who won the Lord Arthur Cecil Memorial Cup at the London Pony Show as a Dales pony. Photo, Charlton Collection.

From 1920, "Glengarry... will not be allowed to compete for the Ministry Premiums in the Appleby or Shap Districts in consequence of the number of years [he and Dalesman] have travelled those Districts."

Glengarry sired RB Charlton's 13-hand Dales mare 3775 Robinson's Gipsy (above), who was shown very successfully from 1922 onward and was the dam of the Fell mare 5902 Linnel Roma who produced Linnel Romany II 2400 (photo, p112). According to the Stud Book, Gipsy and Glengarry were behind 100% of the 2017 and 2018 Fell pony foals.

Glengarry also sired several other Linnel Fell ponies including Linnel Boy 1260 (out of 3722 Linnel Fancy) and 4894 Linnel Coquette (out of 2916 Linnel Flirt). Linnel Fancy and Linnel Flirt are featured in *Magnificent Mares* (p110 *ff*).

Sketch of 6481 Linnel Gipsy Queen, a grand-daughter of Robinson's Gipsy, drawn by Lionel Edwards. Gipsy Queen was dam of Windsor Gipsy (Railton Gipsy Black Princess bred by Mrs Railton in Derbyshire, later bought by King George V and driven by Princesses Margaret and Elizabeth). FPS postcard, with office address at Riccarton Mill, Newcastleton. Courtesy of Christine Morton.

Black Jock II 2321 & Master John 2883 f.1946 - black

Joe Baxter with Master John, Champion at the FPS Stallion Show at Penrith and awarded the Lady Yule Challenge Cup. The prize ticket states that the Show date was Tuesday 13th May 1958.

Master John was Champion at the Stallion Show in 1958, 1960, and 1961. Photo in the Hardman Collection, Kendal (Museum of Lakeland Life and Industry)

Black Jock II's influence on the Fell breed comes through his son Master John 2883 (above). Black Jock's line traced back through the Dales Black Prince II 1809 / Black Diamond 1635 / Staggs Fell Hero / Young Surprise who may have been one of the 15hh cob-like utility horses of the Borders whose blood also contributed to the modern Clydesdale.

Master John was bred in 1946 by James Wilson, Litz Garth (Litts Garth), Stainmore, out of Dainty Molly, by Seldom Seen. His second owner was Joe Baxter of Guardhouse, Threlkeld, shown here at Penrith after winning the Stallion Show with Master John, who had previously held the Travelling Premium in 1952.

Master John was equally well known as a sire of Dales ponies when owned by Mr Joseph Hall, and shown by Walter Tuer of Kirkby Stephen.

Master John's line continued via Heltondale Hero (opposite page) and his son Heltondale Lucky Lad II FP74C*.

Lucky Lad II's son Drybarrows Jeff FP50048C* left 61 foals, mainly for Townend, but also for Carrock, Sleddale and Peepings.

Heltondale Hero 6908 f.1977 - black (Master John / Black Jock II)

Sarge Noble at Butterwick with Heltondale Hero 6908 f.1977, by Heltondale Heather Lad 5493 out of 13938 Heltondale Rosie II; Hero was of the Master John line, going back through Htd Heather Lad to Glenwelt 4546 / Merry John III 3709 to Master John 2883. Photo, FPS Archives / Mrs Greta Noble

Htd Rover III 5875 f.1971, black, by Htd Heather Lad 5493 out of Htd Dolly III 13322; he carried the influence of Master John in his male line, and Htd Romer (Mountain Ranger) in his female line. Photo, FPS Archives

Mighty Atom 382 f.1902 - black

Mighty Atom was bred by William Bowman, at Swindale Foot, Shap. Atom was sired by the brown stallion Jolly Sir John out of Bess, a Fell pony by Eclipse (Fell) out of Polly (Fell); Polly was by a stallion intriguingly named Broken Leg, and out of a mare bred by John Lowis, Rayside, Shap.

Mighty Atom stood 13.2 hands, and as a three-year-old in 1905 he was awarded the Polo and Riding Pony Society's Silver Medal at Westmorland and Kendal Agricultural Society Show, probably in the ownership of Mr Bromley-Wilson of Dallam Tower, Milnthorpe.

I have not found any images of Mighty Atom or of his direct male progeny. However, as the sire of one mare, the grey Flora III (see *Magnificent Mares*), he is represented in all modern pedigrees.

Photo, FPS papers in the Cumbria County Archives, Kendal

HIGH STANDARD OF FELL PONIES

"From our special correspondent" in

The Times, 13 May 1953.

The annual stallion and colt show of the Fell Pony Society, held at Penrith today, again gave much encouragement to those concerned with this hardy moorland breed. Not only were entries slightly more than in 1952, but every animal entered paraded before the judges. ...

The general quality augured well for the future of a breed which is still in demand for utility work on the hill farms of the Lake district and north-west England. ...

For the third successive year the Lady Yule Cup went to Mr W Winder of Caldbeck with his 5-year-old stallion Mountain Model, which has never yet been beaten in the show ring. ... (see p47)

For the fifty-fourth year Mr Baxter had a stallion selected for travelling. This time it was his three-year-old Merry Tom, by his Storm Boy out of Gypsy Queen. Another son of Storm Boy, Guards Hero, was selected as reserve stallion for the Berrier enclosure. ... (see p77)

... the two-year-olds were led by yet another Storm Boy colt, Roundthwaite Lucky Jim, which appeared in the show ring for the first time. (see p149)

STALLIONS OF 1950 ONWARD

Waverhead Rambler 4101 f.1959 - black

Clive Richardson

Jim Bell was six years old when his father John bought him his first Fell pony out of Wigton Auction Mart. John Bell had bred Fell ponies for many years under his Bankhouse prefix and O' the Hill suffix, but it was not until 1946 when Jim married and moved to Waverhead, a hill farm 970 feet above sea level, that his father gave him three mares, Bankhouse Polly, Jewel O' the Hill and Jenny O' the Hill, to establish his own stud.

Left, Rambler's sire Black Grouse 3733 f.1953, by Tebay Little John 3429 out of Snip.
Right, Rambler's dam 8887 Jenny O'the Hill f.1946, by Storm Boy 2288 out of Darky (by Mountain Jester 1409). Bred by Newton Rigg Farm School. Photos courtesy of Barbara Bell & Hilary Lightfoot.

In those days Joe Baxter of Threlkeld travelled a Fell stallion, Storm Boy, in the region and Storm Boy's progeny out of Jim's three mares formed the foundation of a long female line at Waverhead which continues to this day. However, as the old tradition of travelling stallions began to die out Jim decided to keep his own stallion. He went to visit Ted Benson in 1959 and bought a two year old colt, Adamthwaite Lucky Star. The following year Lucky Star was champion at the Fell Pony Stallion Show held in those days at Myers Lane in Penrith. At that time the Fell Pony Society used to run an enclosure scheme whereby a tract of land was

Adamthwaite Lucky Star with mares on the Berrier Enclosure. FPS Archives

rented for the breeding season and members voted for the stallion they would like to run on the enclosure and to which they could take their mares for a nominal fee.

In the late 1950s Jim also sent a number of mares up to Neil Manning's stallion, Black Grouse, which ran on high ground around the Devil's Beef Tub near Moffat. One of the resulting foals out of Jenny O'the Hill, one of Jim's original foundation mares, was a colt named Waverhead Rambler, foaled in 1959. He was the first homebred Waverhead colt to be retained, and became one of the most influential stallions in the breed.

Although Rambler won the championship at the Fell Pony Stallion Show on a number of occasions, it was his prepotency or ability to pass on his own qualities with consistency to his foals that stamped his progeny, which ensured a dynasty of ponies at Waverhead whose style is still evident today in his many descendants all over the country and abroad.

Not surprisingly many other breeders were keen to avail themselves of Rambler for their own mares. Rambler ran on the Caldbeck Enclosure for the seasons 1966 and 1968, making him accessible to many members and spreading his bloodline through the breed.

In 1969 the National Pony Society organised a display of native ponies at the Horse of the Year Show at Wembley to raise awareness of the diversity of native breeds. Each display stand was to house a mare and foal and a stallion, and Waverhead Rambler was the stallion that was selected to represent the breed. The background to the stand was painted by Peggy Crossland, secretary of the Society at that time, and represented a Lake District scene, while wallpaper

Waverhead Rambler 4101 f.1959, by Black Grouse 3733 out of 8887 Jenny O'the Hill.
This photo was taken at the NPS Show in 1969 when Rambler represented the Fell pony breed in the Native Pony exhibit. Photo, courtesy of Barbara Bell & Hilary Lightfoot.

printed with a dry stone wall design covered the pen front and a large potted Scotch thistle added authenticity. (After the event the thistle was planted behind the stadium and self-seeded everywhere). The stand won the silver medal and, more significantly, helped publicise the Fell breed to a much wider audience.

At the first Fell Pony Breed Show in 1970, one of Rambler's daughters, Waverhead Peggy, won the championship, and in subsequent years other Rambler progeny took the coveted title on several occasions including Waverhead Honour in 1971 and Peggy again in 1972 when her full sister, Waverhead Mayfly, won the Columbine cup for the best ridden mare. Both Peggy and Mayfly also won the Fell championship for the Bell family at the Royal Show. Another Fell Pony Society Breed Show champion by Rambler was Waverhead Gypsy. In the 1970s it was not unusual to have three or four groups of ponies all sired by Rambler but exhibited by different breeders in the stallion progeny class. One year there were fifteen of Rambler's progeny at the Breed Show where three of them, Waverhead Peggy, Waverhead Mayfly and Waverhead Robin, won the Lady Yule cup for the best group of three.

Waverhead Peggy. Photo, courtesy of Barbara Bell & Hilary Lightfoot.

Other Rambler sons and daughters winning consistently at shows up and down the country included Waverhead Magic, whose many wins included winning the Fell class at the Royal Windsor Show four times as well as the supreme Mountain and Moorland championship in 1976. She was successfully shown under saddle and in harness driven to a dogcart and after being retired to stud she bred Waverhead Prince II (by Greenholme Geoff 6747) who over his stud career sired 177 progeny.

In 2000 at the age of seventeen Waverhead Prince II was champion at the Fell Pony Society Stallion Show (opposite, top right). One of Prince II's sons, Waverhead Dazzler, went on to have a very successful ridden career as well as carrying the bloodline forward.

Among Rambler's many other notable progeny was Waverhead Model, a full brother to Waverhead Magic, Waverhead Peggy and Waverhead Mayfly; all were out of Townend Polly VIII. Model returned to the Bell family ownership later in his career and was successfully used. Another Rambler son, Waverhead Rob, was influential at Jane Glass' Wolds Stud in Leicestershire, while Waverhead Fury was bought by the Miss Brookes for their stud near Peebles and also used by Elizabeth Ball at her Barncrosh Stud in Dumfries. Rambler's many daughters included Waverhead Polly and Waverhead Molly, both hugely successful in ridden classes, Waverhead Julie whose show ring successes were carried on by her daughter, Robbswater Ruth, and Border Black Empress, four times ridden champion at the Breed Show.

Occasionally, Jim Bell would buy in a mare related to his own bloodline to introduce a splash of fresh blood. One such pony was Barbondale Petal, bred by Alan Shuttleworth and out of Waverhead Jewel, a Rambler granddaughter, by Waverhead Model. Jewel as a yearling had been youngstock champion at the Breed Show as well as youngstock champion at the Royal Show. Petal was a prolific winner in the show ring before being retired to stud. Petal's daughter, Waverhead Jubilee, is the mother of

Waverhead Prince II. Photo, courtesy of Barbara Bell & Hilary Lightfoot.

Waverhead Skylark, one of the current brood mares at Waverhead where she has a fine filly foal by Waverfoot Gary bred by Barbara's niece, Hilary Lightfoot. Petal's half-sister, Barbondale Pearl, out of Waverhead Jewel but by Townend Bracken, again purchased from Alan Shuttleworth, bred many good foals by Waverhead Model for the Bells and her bloodline continues in ponies currently at Waverhead.

Another purchase was Redhouse Dusty, also by Rambler, and one of the most admired ridden ponies of her day. Dusty's son, Waverhead Copper, and his sister, Waverhead Dusty, both headed south to new owners, as did so many of Rambler's second generation progeny who went on to make names for themselves with other owners and breeders. Jim Bell had been a member of the Fell Pony Society since joining aged 16 in 1938 and remained a

Waverhead Model at the FPS Stallion show with Nancy Lightfoot. Photo, courtesy of Barbara Bell & Hilary Lightfoot.

member for the next 64 years. In the 70s and 80s he, his wife Frances, and daughters Nancy and Barbara, had showed their ponies at around 15 shows a year on average. They often took a full wagonload to a show with entries in most classes and they enjoyed consistent success wherever they went. The death of Nancy in a tragic road accident in 1998 was a huge loss to the family and they curtailed their showing activities as a result.

Following the deaths of Jim and Frances, Barbara has kept the stud going with help from Hilary and, although their showing activities are not on the scale they once were, their occasional forays into the show ring are usually met with great success. Moreover, the many descendants of Rambler scattered across the country as well as in Europe and America ensure that the legacy of this outstanding stallion will continue for many generations to come.

Waverhead Rambler, champion at the Stallion Show in 1968. Jim Bell receives the Lady Yule Cup from FPS President Major Hasell. Photo in the Herald, by Eric Davidson.
Clipping courtesy of Sue Howes

Waverhead Rambler, courtesy of Sue Howes. He sired a total of 57 foals.

Gibside Danny Boy 6458, by Waverhead Rambler 4101 out of 12047 Linnel Madam. Photo, Ruth Eastwood

Waverhead Copper, FP50998C* f.1999, dark brown, by Lownthwaite Gary FP825C* out of FP1198* Redhouse Dusty. Ridden by Laura Barsoum, he was Champion at the Southern Breed Show in 2011.

Photo, FPS Magazine

The Stallions on the Enclosures 1945-73

Year	Location	Stallion	% in modern pedigrees*
1945	The Nettles	Linnel Raven II	100%
		(assumed from registrations in 1946)	
1945	The Nettles	Linnel Romany II	<25%
1948	Berrier	Heltondale Romer	100%
1950	High Arnside	Rowland Boy	<25%
1950	Berrier	Linnel Osprey	100%
1951	High Arnside	Park House Victor	100%
1951	Berrier	Mountain Model	100%
1952	Berrier	Mountain Model	100%
1952	Windermere, Crag House	Park House Victor	100%
1953	Berrier	Mountain Model	100%
1953	Windermere, Crag House	Park House Victor	100%
1959	Coniston	Packway Royal	100%
1966	Caldbeck	Waverhead Rambler	100%
1967	Sleddale	Heltondale Sonny Boy	100%
1968	Caldbeck	Waverhead Rambler	100%
1968	Sleddale	Heltondale Sonny Boy	100%
1972	Caldbeck	Baldersdale Hero	<25%
1972	Dowthwaite Head	Dene Beau Banner	0%
1972	Reserve	Lunesdale Richard	100%
1973	Dowthwaite Head	Baldersdale Hero	<25%

*I am indebted to Jenifer Morrissey for the above data, and she adds this caveat: "Percentages are based on the pedigrees published in the stud books of the Fell Pony Society, which rely on breeders for accuracy."

Travelling Premiums

1950-51 Storm Boy 2288
1952   Master John 2883
1953   Merry Tom 3138

At Home Premiums: examples

1950	Dalemain Groundsel 2703
1951	Blake Beck Boy 2842
	Stouphill Mountain Boy 2756
1952	Glendramackin 3259
	Hutton Nomad 2933
1953	Blake Beck Boy 2842
	Hutton Nomad 2933
	Adamthwaite Warrior 4439
	Adamthwaite Lucky Star 4067
	Roundthwaite Lucky Jim 3258

An example of the hand-written records from 1953 when Park House Victor stood at Crag House, Windermere. Mares included Guards Daisy, Linnel Buzzard, Sleddale Rose II, Sleddale Rose III, Sleddale Beauty, Gay Lady of Fairfield. Two colt foals and two filly foals are recorded with them, all by Park House Victor. Photo, FPS archive in County Archives, Kendal

Mr Richard Little's stallion Guards Hero 2987, by Storm Boy 2288 out of 8855 Guards Peggy. Champion at the Stallion Show in 1954 and subsequently sold to the Government of Pakistan to improve stock there.

Townend Flash II 5278 f.1969 - black

*Above, Townend Flash II with his breeder Eddie Wilson and his winnings
in just one of his highly successful seasons. Below, with Glenis Wilson. Photos, FPS Archives.*

Flash was shown both in hand and under saddle by Eddie Wilson's daughter Glenis (left and opposite page) who now breeds using the Carrock prefix. Photo, FPS Archives

By Lunesdale Richard 4637 out of 10976 Townend Polly VI, Townend Flash II traced through his sire to Heltondale Prince and the Mountain Ranger line.

On his dam's side Flash came from a line of good Townend ponies, Polly IV 9472 and Polly III 8248, back to the stallions Black Jock II and Bob Silvertail (Weardale Hero / Teesdale Comet / Comet II line). Lunesdale Richard's dam Lunesdale Peggy was a good quality Inspected mare who was granted full breeding status a year or so before the grading-up scheme was brought in.

Townend Flash II won the Championship at the Stallion Show 9 times between 1974 and 1983, a clear indication of his popularity and quality, and he sired a total of 99 foals. He was behind 51% of foals in the 2005 and 2006 foal crops, according to the Stud Books, and 67% of foals in 2017 and 2018.

Townend Flash II being shown by Margaret Wilson at the stallion Show at Yanwath Wood, Lowther, in 1982. Photo, FPS Archives, taken by Greta Noble

Tebay Campbellton Victor 6614* f.1976 - black

Lynn Trotter with her father's stallion TC Victor, at Ravenstonedale Show, probably in 1979 when he won a youngstock class. Photo, Marilyn Darcy.

Victor was bred in 1976 by David Trotter of Tebay, by Lownthwaite Star Dust 5965 out of 15877 Tebay Brandy. His name appears in several different forms due to typographical variations in the Stud Book: Campbell Ton, Campbelltown, Cambellton and Campbellton. The form given here, "Campbellton" is what his breeder always insisted it should be.

Victor was used in his youth by his breeder at Tebay, not only because he was such a good stamp of pony, but because David had only used the sire, L. Star Dust, on two of his mares, so Victor carried lines that were mostly unrelated to the rest of the herd. Through Heltondale Sonny Boy he traced strongly to Mountain Ranger (through Htd Romer being close up in that pedigree four times), and on his dam's side he descended from Master John through the grandsire and to an Inspected mare 12941 Heltondale Mary (I.S.).

After a few years at Tebay Victor went to Sarge Noble, Heltondale; later David bought him back and used him, and finally he returned to Sarge once more. Many of his early progeny were not registered as he was not licensed until he was 7 or 8 years old; David Trotter said he could easily sell the ponies on their quality alone, and his buyers were not interested in the paperwork. It was his daughter Lynn's insistence that made sure Victor was licensed. He was very rarely shown, although he won a class at Ravenstonedale as a 3 year old, and paraded at the FPS Stallion show in the 1990s.

Victor's last foal was born in 2001. David Trotter went to visit Sarge Noble around this time and viewed a line of ponies standing in a building. When "a nice little grey one" looked at him and whickered in recognition he was surprised to find it was Victor, by then showing his advanced age but still remembering David and, possibly, their days when David used to ride him up the fell to gather the herd. Despite his small size he was a very useful mount when doing this job because he knew the fell, having been born there, and being entire he was always willing to find the mares quickly!

Tebay Campbellton Victor, aged 19, at home with Sarge Noble at Bampton. Photo, Mrs Greta Noble.

Victor was widely used by many studs including Gaisgill (George Winder), Greenholme (Bill Potter), Murthwaite (Thomas Capstick) and Wellbrow (Andrew Thorpe). None of them used him exclusively; they used other stallions of the time as well. However, David Trotter said of him, "It didn't matter what sort of mare you put to him, he threw that quality to it.

Tebay Vespa FP779G f.1986 by TC Victor out of 16971 Tebay Startrek; in costume for a period drama. Photo, courtesy of Alison O'Neill

Heather Lad, that we had in the early '80s, he was a nice pony but he didn't stamp his stock the way Victor did. You could tell his get anywhere; they were like peas in a pod."

"He was 12.2, and built like a brick ... he was a good looker in his own way. When he went to the summer breed show as a yearling he was in a class of his own, as far as feather was concerned, and bone. Although I never owned him, I have quite a lot of ponies got by him. These Victor mares seemed to click with Black Prince and his stock, although they were two completely different types of stallion. One of the best getters was Victor." (Thomas Capstick)

Examples of successful stallions by Victor

Tebay Vespa FP779G f.1986 out of 16971 Tebay Startrek, breeder David Trotter.

Known at home as Boxer, Vespa sired 84 foals for the Tebay, Murthwaite and Gaisgill studs before he was gelded in 1992. He was a beautiful pony but very opinionated. He became a working pony for Alison O'Neill, and after a battle of wills that included a broken arm for Alison, she used him for shepherding and carriage-driving, and he even took part in a historical TV drama (see previous page).

Wellbrow Leo FP50513C* f.1996 out of 18068 Heltondale Polly Perkins IV, breeder Andrew Thorpe.

Leo sired 86 foals, mostly for Wellbrow but also for Stunstead (Harrison/Richardson) and Charellbre (Misses Fletcher).

Sleddale Eddie FP50762C* f.1997 by Murthwaite Victor FP652G* (by TC Victor) out of FP1003 Sleddale Lib. Eddie went to The Netherlands and has 17 progeny in various parts of Europe and North America.

Examples of Victor progeny out of mares by Htd Black Prince III

FP3859* Carltonlima Emma by TC Victor out of FP1774* Heltondale Daisy IV, breeder Mr R Sandham; dam's sire Htd Black Prince III. Emma was a long-term regular mount for HM The Queen's morning rides and has had one foal for the Balmoral stud.

FP3345 Heltondale Magic XIV by TC Victor out of Htd Magic VIII; dam's sire Htd Black Prince III (Magic had 4 foals).

FP3147 Murthwaite Greta by TC Victor out of FP1692* Greenholme Dusty; dam's sire Htd Black Prince III (Greta had 3 foals).

FP2878 Heltondale Misty IV by TC Victor out of FP1692* Greenholme Dusty, breeder Sarge Noble; dam's sire Htd Black Prince III. (Misty had 5 foals, including FP4990 Murthwaite Ripley, see following pages).

FP2878 Heltondale Misty IV f.1996, by TC Victor out of FP1692* Greenholme Dusty, breeder Sarge Noble; dam's sire Htd Black Prince III. Owner, Thomas Capstick. Photo, FPS Magazine

Murthwaite

Heltondale Misty IV f.1996, black, by TC Victor out of FP1692 Greenholme Dusty. Owned and exhibited by Thomas Capstick. Photo, FPS Magazine, Anthony Reynolds*

Among many other successes, Misty won the 2007 Olympia Ridden Qualifier at the FPS Breed show, and at the 2008 Breed Show she was doubly reserve Champion, for Mares and Overall.

FP3291 Murthwaite Mulan f.1998, also by TC Victor out of FP1692* Greenholme Dusty, breeder Thomas Capstick. Also multiple times a champion.

Misty's full sister, the 2002 Breed Show Champion FP3291 Murthwaite Mulan f.1998. Their dam's sire was Htd Black Prince III. Owned and exhibited by Thomas Capstick. Photo, FPS Magazine

Murthwaite Look at Me FP51001C* f.1999 - black

Thomas Capstick's stallion Murthwaite Look at Me FP51001C f.1999, (by Heltondale Bobby FP644C* by TC Victor) out of FP2054* Greenholme Jess, (by Htd. Black Prince III). Champion Stallion (above, when he was aged 3) at the FPS Stallion and Colt Show for three years running, 2002, 2003, 2004. Photo, Sue Millard*

Greenholme Look at Me FP70294C f.2003, by Murthwaite Look At Me FP51001C* out of FP3063 Greenholme Petal, at the Stallion Show in 2007, shown by John Potter. G Look at Me has 76 progeny. Photo, Joanne Exley*

Heltondale Black Prince III f. 1982 - black

Bill Potter and Thomas Capstick with Black Prince III, in 1992 at the Stallion Show, where Prince was champion 4 times between 1990 and 1994. Photo, Roy Wallis.

Black Prince's influence on the breed has been discussed in previous chapters and examples of the quality of his offspring, especially when crossed with those of TC Victor, have been shown in the preceding pages. Prince's 232 progeny would fill a book by themselves so I will restrain myself and just add this early photo of him by Roy Wallis who kindly gave it to me some years ago to be added to the FPS Archive.

As a measure of Prince's lasting popularity, the At Home Premiums given by the Fell Pony Society tell the story very clearly in the Newsletter reports:

1988: Every year the Fell Pony Society awards up to six premiums of £30 each for the stallions serving the highest number of registered Fell mares, and this year's winners were -

    Mr. W. S. Noble's Heltondale Black Prince III (29 mares)

    Mr. J. Bell's Waverhead Prince II (11 mares)

    Mrs. J. Hutchinson's Tarnmoor Prince (8 mares)

Ten years later, in 1998:

    Mr. W. S. Noble's Heltondale Black Prince III (28 mares)

    Miss J. Glass' Baronshill Indiana Jones (7 mares)

    Mr. E. M. Wilson's Heltondale Duke (23 mares)

Bill Potter and Thomas Capstick went into a partnership to buy and use Prince on their Greenholme and Murthwaite mares.

Prince was eventually sold out of the UK, in 1995: there were so many ponies sired by him that, as they came to breeding age, it was difficult to avoid kin-breeding/line-breeding. And although the Foal Immunodeficiency Syndrome had not been named and a carrier test had not yet been found, Prince was one of several stallions known to have sired FIS foals.

Barbara Muller bought him for her Narnia stud in northern Germany, where he ended his days at the age of 30 as a family friend and a grand ambassador for the breed in Europe.

Performing with the FPS Display Team at Black Combe Country Fair in 2016:

(on the right) Cath Wrigley riding FP4990 Murthwaite Ripley, by FP51001C* Murthwaite Look At Me (above) out of Htd Misty IV (facing page, top). Victor and Black Prince III each occur twice in the first 3 generations of Ripley's pedigree.

On the left, Georgia Ellis on homebred Harthouse Hillman FP71338G.

Photo, Simon Ellis.

Murthwaite Windrush FP51201C*by FP50539C* - Murthwaite Bross out of FP2054* - Greenholme Jess (by Htd Black Prince III), Stallion Show Champion in 2013. Photo, FPS Magazine, by Fleur Hallam

Mr & Mrs Colin Turner's Murthwaite Gurkha FP70591G* by Murthwaite Look At Me FP51001C*
out of FP2133 Heltondale Dainty VI, by Heltondale Rover IV FP480C; champion at the 2009
Derbyshire FPS Show. Photo, FPS Magazine

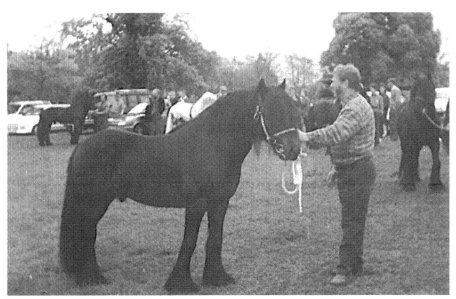

Heltondale Ted FP487C*, brown, f.1987, by Heltondale Black Prince III FP188C* out of FP1008*
Adamthwaite Bell Heather, seen here at the Stallion Show, owned and exhibited by Bill Potter. Htd
Ted had 74 progeny. Photo, courtesy of Bill & Isobel Potter.

Murthwaite Black Bobby FP50558G, f.1996, by Heltondale Bobby FP644C*(by Tebay Campbellton Victor 6641) out of FP2051 Tebay Blackbird (also by TC Victor). Photo courtesy of Bill & Isobel Potter*

Greenholme Ringo FP51020C (dark brown) f.1999, by Greenholme Mikado FP50337C* (by Murthwaite Victor) out of FP2052 Greenholme Jacklynne (by Htd Ted). Photo courtesy of Bill & Isobel Potter*

Greenholme Warbler FP70489C* f2004, by Linnel Reynard FP708C* out of FP1895 Tebay Duchess (by TC Victor 6614). Winner of the 3 and 4 year old class at the 2007 stallion show. At the time he was owned jointly by George Guy with Paul Metcalfe (exhibiting). He is now owned by Cath Wigley. Photo, FPS Magazine

A Warbler daughter: FP5351 Hedgethorpe June Delight f.2010, by Greenholme Warbler FP70489C* out of FP3634 Hedgethorpe April Morning (by Severnvale Hector). Owned and shown by Tara Robinson, winner of the Mountain and Moorland In Hand class at NPS in 2019 and Reserve Champion. Photo, FPS Mazazine, Sally Coles.

Greenholme Warrior FP70490C*, f.2004, by Lunesdale Redstart FP50708C* out of FP3281 Greenholme Sasha (by Greenholme Mikado FP50337C*) at an open day at Stony Ghyll for the Society's 90th anniversary in 2012. Photo, Joanne Bennett

A Warrior son: Greenholme Elect FP71650C*f.2010, by Greenholme Warrior FP70490C* out of FP4509 Greenholme Amie Good Un, at the Stallion show in 2014, with Rob Relph-Briggs.
Photo, FPS Magazine

Greenholme Diego FP71371C* f.2009, by Greenholme Look At Me FP70294C* (by Murthwaite Look at Me) out of FP4102 Greenholme What Do U Think (by Lunesdale Redstart FP50708C*) reserve Supreme Champion at the Stallion show in 2019, exhibited by John Potter. Photo, FPS Magazine, Form & Function Photography

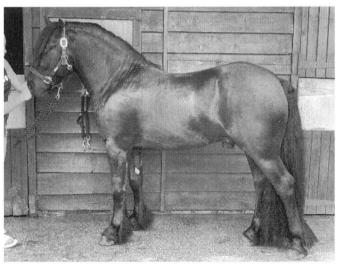

"A good colt makes a good gelding" - A Diego son, Greenholme Luke FP72771G, f.2017, by Greenholme Diego FP71371C* (by Greenholme Look at Me, see page 84) out of FP3899 Salisbury Delia (by Lownthwaite Gary FP825C*), owned by Miss Emily Webster. Photo, FPS Magazine

Wellbrow

Wellbrow Lancashire Lad FP71670C* f.2010, by Heltondale Mountain Mist II FP50429C* out of FP4060 Wellbrow Ruby. Seen here as a 2 year-old in 2012 during the FPS 90th Anniversary. Among those viewing Lancashire Lad are: Katherine Savage, Ali and Isabel Slack, Christine Robinson, Mary Longsdon. Photo, Joanne Bennett.

Wellbrow Express FP71972G f.2011, by Heltondale Mountain Mist II FP50429C* out of FP3570 Wellbrow Rona (by Townend Henry FP44C*) shown by Gemma Thorpe; yearling class winner at the Stallion show in 2012. Photo, FPS Magazine, Fleur Hallam.

Wellbrow Black Jack FP70462C* by Heltondale Mountain Mist II FP50429C* out of FP3277 Wellbrow Dolly, at Great Yorkshire Show 2013, owned and shown by Hayley Martin. Judge, Russell Sutcliffe. Photo, FPS Magazine

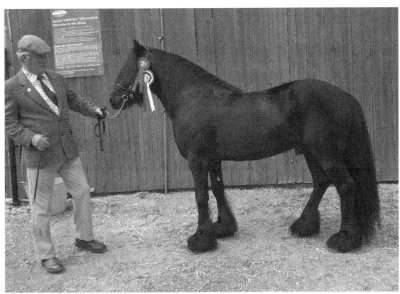

Andrew Thorpe's Wellbrow Mikado FP72283C* f.2013, by FP50429C* Heltondale Mountain Mist II out of FP3537 Wellbrow Carmen (by FP50337C* Greenholme Mikado). Champion Fell at the Great Yorkshire Show, 2016. Photo, FPS Magazine

Rackwood

Rackwood Prince FP523C* f.1988, by Townend Henry FP44C* out of 18034* Rackwood Dewdrop. Bred by Mr GR Coatsworth. Stallion Show, 1990s. Photo Roy Wallis

Example of Prince's progeny: Gowbarrow Henry FP50210G, with breeder Ruth Eastwood. By Rackwood Prince FP523C* out of FP1370 Bluecaster Gracie Grundy.
Photo, courtesy of Ruth Eastwood

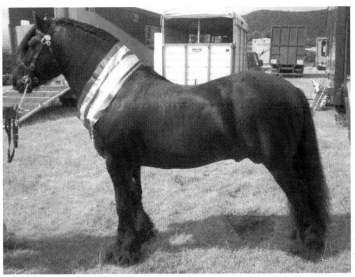

Jenny Crane's stallion Rackwood Robin FP923C* f.1992, by Whinbush Robin FP418C out of 18034* Rackwood Dewdrop, winning the M&M Home Produced final and the Supreme In-hand Championship at the NPS Summer Championships. Photo, FPS Photo Gallery

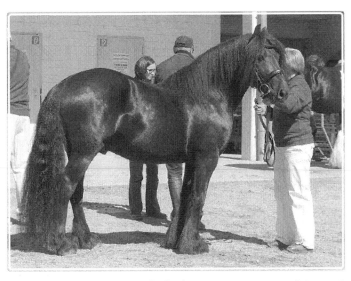

Rackwood Amos FP71830C* f.2011, by Brackenbank Amos FP71039C* out of FP4418* Rackwood Melody. Amos was 1st prize foal at his first two shows when shown with his dam and M&M Champion at his first three foal shows after weaning. He is now a licensed stallion in Germany.
Photo, courtesy of Eileen Walker

Lunesdale

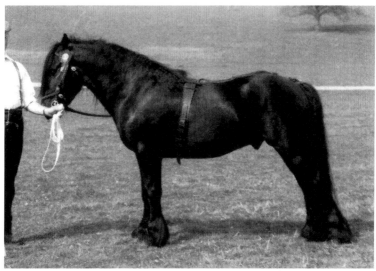

Lunesdale Charles FP19C, f.1980, by Lunesdale Jerry 6841 out of 17842 Lunesdale Beauty III, seen here at the Stallion and Colt Show at Dalemain in 1984. There is more about the Lunesdale Ponies in the Mares section. Photo, FPS Archives

Lunesdale Warlord FP71091C* f.2007, by Greenholme Warrior FP70490C* out of FP3455 Lunesdale Lady Rebecca. As a 2-year-old in 2009 (above) Warlord was Youngstock Champion and Overall Supreme Champion at the Stallion and Colt Show at Dalemain. He has 49 progeny to date.

There is more about his dam and grand-dam in the Mares section. Photo, Joanne Exley

A STALLION MISCELLANY

The sires of these ponies may be in the previous chapters, and their dams are likely to be in the following ones.

Townend Prince III 5680 f.1971, by Htd Sonny Boy 4473 out of 12828 Waverhead Princess. Photo, FPS Archives, Courtesy of John Slater/Margaret Bainbridge, former groom with Beth Slater at Mr RWT Bray's Greenfield Stud.

Peter Lawson's Mountain Dew of Cleveland 6976 f.1975, by Frizington White Heather 4209 out of 14967 Scarhead Betty (by Lownthwaite Fire 4808). He was Champion Stallion in 1984, shown by Sheena Lawson. He had 11 progeny. Photo, FPS Magazine Archive

Greenfield Gay Lad 544C* f.1979 (Tebay Thunder 6338 x 15011 Greenfield Faerie Queen), seen here in 2009, at the grand age of 30. He was Supreme Champion at the Stallion and colt show in 1988, shown by Mr. C. Howarth. Photo, Joanne Exley

For comparison, Heltondale Ted FP487C* as a 3-year-old, shown by Bill Potter (see p87 for Htd Ted as a mature horse). Clive Richardson (background, far right) judging, at the Stallion & Colt Show at Dalemain, 1990. Photo, Ruth Eastwood.

Mr D Howe's Tunstall Jake FP50777C* f.1998, by Heltondale Bracken V FP50170C* (by Tebay Campbellton Victor) out of FP1958 Tunstall Beauty IV (by Townend Bracken III 6020). At the Stallion Show in 2000 or thereabouts. Photo, Courtesy of Bill & Isobel Potter (photo, Mr & Mrs Kell)

Drybarrows Cosmopolitan FP72863C* f.2017, by Carrock I'm Yer Man FP51327C* out of FP4317 Drybarrows Fern. Youngstock Champion at the 2019 Stallion Show. Owner Mr M Cornthwaite, breeder Mr D Thompson. Photo, FPS Magazine, Form and Function Photography

Bracklinn Jackpot FP71036C* f.2007, by Carrock I'm Yer Man FP51327C* out of FP2162 Southolme Beauty, Champion at the FPS Stallion Show in 2011 with owner breeder Alistair Smith.
Photo, Ruth Eastwood

Linnel Rapier 2825 f.1948, by Linnel Lingcropper 1621 out of 5902 Linnel Roma, 1st prize at the Royal Show in 1955, and best of all breeds.

FELL COMMONS AND RIGHTS TO GRAZE FELL PONIES

Sue Millard

Fell rights are vital to our hill breeders in Cumbria and Lancashire, and so this article was proposed in FPS Council in July 2019. As Magazine Editor, I took responsibility for compiling the information.

This article is not a statement of law. It is a brief overview of commons and rights, to try to shed some light on how the fell commons work, and to explain why the pony herds which run on the commons remain relatively few in number. Admittedly, the overall picture is not always easy to understand. Even people who own property with fell rights may only be familiar with the law for their own area, and those rights vary between different commons. I have talked to several Fell pony breeders, all of whom have experience of running ponies on shared commons. Some of them have advised or dealt with the Department for the Environment, Food and Rural Affairs (DEFRA) or Natural England (NE). Most preferred not to be named here.

There is a great deal of information available online, such as Government Guidance on Managing Common Land, the DEFRA Database of Common Land, Commons Registers, Common Land Grazing Rights (for farm subsidies), Commons Associations and Federations.

I have given numbered references throughout to the places where I found the information here, from books and from online sources. Please use the numbers in the text to find the references listed at the end (p216). However, new legislation is pending in the form of the Environmental Land Management Scheme, for which Government web sites such as DEFRA's Future Farming blog will need to be consulted.

History & Tradition

The origins of common land-use are extremely ancient, because woodland, riversides, marshes, moors, downlands, peat bogs and "wastes" were all important local resources. The "open field" system of agriculture provided each family with its own strip of land near the village to grow vegetables, fruits and grain. Milking cattle, goats and sheep, working oxen and horses grazed together on a large communal meadow within walking distance of the village. Other livestock were turned onto the common land beyond the meadow. These could have included heifers and dry cows; wether sheep, and ewes with lambs; geese; goats; and - of most interest from our point of view - the young horses or ponies, breeding mares, or horses or ponies not in work. *(Fowler, 2002, i)*

Access to the common land was shared out among the people who lived in the village, and the resulting "rights" were overseen by its Manor Court. One of the last surviving working examples of this ancient management system in England is at Orton (Cumbria), where our

FPS AGM is held. Laxton in Nottinghamshire still has a court and a working open field system; the New Forest has monthly court meetings.

The point about fell rights is that they shared out the village's grazing on a reasonable basis. "Common land" then did not mean "public access". It meant that although the Lord(s) of the Manor owned the land, the grazing and other rights were held by villagers "in common" - ie, by the people as a group.

However, various Enclosures Acts from the 17th century onward enabled rich families to fence off common land and turn it into private property (*iii*).

The first parliamentary enclosure act, dating from 1767, was for 158 acres on Kendal Fell. An act to enclose a substantial area at Orton was passed in 1769, but took 10 years to accomplish because of "major problems" (*ii*). 91 people in the parish of Ravenstonedale had also signed a petition which successfully opposed an attempt by Sir James Lowther, as the lord of the manor, to enclose the commons. However Bolton, near Appleby, preferred to enclose its common to prevent overgrazing by cattle being droved south from Scotland.

The destruction of the ancient system was a huge shock to rural communities, as pithily outlined in this verse of an old poem:

> *The law locks up the man or woman*
> *Who steals the goose from off the common,*
> *But leaves the greater villain loose*
> *Who steals the common from the goose.*

Principal beneficiaries during enclosures in Westmorland were the Earls of Thanet and Earls of Lonsdale, who were possibly speculating by buying the lordships of commons and enclosing them (*iii*). Parcels or "allotments" of land enclosed from the common were awarded to individuals but also to organisations - churches, chapels, schools, overseers of the poor and private charities, but enclosure did not benefit the majority of country people. Those who could not find work near their villages had to move to an industrial town or city, and labour there – a "country-to-town" drift that is still ongoing today.

The farmers who use their rights today to run sheep, cattle and ponies on fell commons are keeping up a tradition, which is at least a thousand years old, of living intelligently "with" the land.

Commons in England today

The Ministry of Agriculture, Fisheries and Food (MAFF) carried out a biological survey between 1982 and 1993, of common land which had been registered in 1970. In that survey, 7,052 commons were listed in England. *(DEFRA Database of Common Land, iv)* These data form a snapshot of the registers of common land at that time.

The Government defines common land as "land owned by one or more persons where other people, known as 'commoners', are entitled to use the land or take resources from it." *(Government Guidance on Managing Common Land, v)* The Countryside and Rights of Way Act 2000 *(vi)* gave the public the "right to roam" across many of these uncultivated areas, though not to behave recklessly or disturb livestock or wildlife. As an example, 80% of the Howgill Fells is now designated as public access land, one of the highest percentages in England.

In 2001 MAFF was renamed the Department for Environment, Food and Rural Affairs (DEFRA), and it no longer receives amendments to the Commons Registers, so the most up to date versions are now held by local authorities, eg Cumbria Commons Registration Servicevii and Lancashire County Council. *(vi, vii, viii)*

Commons in Cumbria and Lancashire

The Federation of Cumbria Commoners now lists 630 commons in Cumbria (Map of Cumbria's Commons *(ix)*, ranging in size from less than half a hectare to well over 3,000ha. The 5 single largest named commons are Dufton (4,616ha), Coniston/Dunnerdale/Seathwaite (4,552ha), Brackenthwaite (4,256ha), Caldbeck (3,726ha) and Eskdale (3,071ha). In all there are 41 commons over 1,000ha in size, though where commons adjoin one another the tracts of ground are very much larger. These are all on high ground, for example on the Howgills, on the Pennines, and on the High Street ridge between Ullswater and Haweswater.

43 of the commons in Cumbria and 1 in Lancashire are designated as Sites of Special Scientific Interest (SSSIs). 25 commons lay within the Lake District National Park as it was before changes of boundary in 2017.

6 commons are in an Area of Outstanding Natural Beauty, and these are all in the North Pennines AONB.

Databases and Registers of Common Land

Commons with rights to graze horses or ponies

161 commons in Cumbria and Lancashire had fell rights registered to graze horses or ponies, often alongside cattle, sheep, pigs, poultry and goats:

141 commons were registered in Cumbria (129 in Cumberland or Westmorland, and 12 in South Lakeland, "Lancashire north of the Sands")

20 commons in Lancashire.

161 commons in total. *(DEFRA Database of Common Land [2012, data from 1993], x and the Commons Register 2000, xi)*

The 2006 Commons Act

Rights have always varied from common to common because the local laws developed by tradition, from the needs of a particular village or villages, without any overarching legal guidance at national level. The intention in 2006 was to bring the registered rights of 1970 up to date, and theoretically there might then have been an increase in the number of pony grazing rights discovered, proved and registered. However, by 2009 it seems that the process was taking very much longer than had been expected so the target date of 2010 for completion "became unrealistic".

Basic Payment Scheme subsidy

The Rural Payments Agency managed the EU subsidies which were given to farms. No financial support was given directly to animals, whether housed, or in enclosed fields, or on commons. Subsidies were based solely on the land itself. The most recent data I can find about commons are in a PDF document detailing farm Basic Payment Scheme (BPS) claims, made by farmers in 2017 for 2018 payment on the area of land they farmed, including their Common Land Grazing Rights *(xii)*.

These rights are brought into the land calculation as explained below. *(xiii)*

Livestock Units (for BPS)

Up to 2021, graziers claimed BPS subsidy for their share of a common by declaring their Common Land Grazing Rights on it. The process was more complex than claiming directly for their area of enclosed farm land (in-bye fields). A BPS claim for shared grazing on a common was expressed first as rights, then converted to Livestock Units, then translated into hectarage for the purposes of the subsidy claim. *(Commons eligibility checks 2019, xiv)* This is where things become complicated.

The 2018 Livestock Unit values, for farmers to calculate their BPS subsidy claims for common rights, were as follows:

Livestock type	Livestock Unit value
	(BPS Rules 2018, xv)
Cattle	1.00
Horses	1.00
Donkeys	0.60
Heifers or Stirks	0.60
Ponies	0.60
Pigs	0.30
Goats	0.15
Sheep	0.15
Geese	0.04
Poultry (over 6 months)	0.02

Livestock Units (LUs) are purely theoretical. They are used to calculate the nominal area of common land a farm might claim, for its BPS subsidy. They are not the same thing as Common Land Grazing Rights which define what animals can be grazed on the land, and how many. Rights making up (for example) 10 LUs may look as though you could graze 10 horses, or 10 cattle, or 66 sheep, or 16 ponies, but the grazing rights themselves still define what you can graze on a particular fell common.

Applications for farm BPS subsidies reveal that in Cumbria in 2017, only 63 commons were noted as having rights registered for ponies – many fewer than the documented "paper" rights in 1993.

Common Land Grazing Rights

Common Land Grazing Rights are now permanently attached to property; eg, to a house, a farm or a parcel of land.

Commons are subject to agreements with all the commoners who share the grazing, and to any agreements they have signed up to with Natural England (NE). Existing grazing rights are used to calculate BPS subsidy (see previous page).

Theoretically DEFRA and NE might countenance an exchange of sheep or cattle rights for ponies. However that still depends on the existing arrangements for that common, and in practice if there have not been any pony grazing rights registered it is unlikely the other graziers would agree.

Selling or Leasing Common Land Grazing Rights

You can only sell rights these days by selling them with land or property, unless you are selling or transferring them to either Natural England or a Commons Council, or anyone named in an order made by the Secretary of State for Environment, Food and Rural Affairs.

Grazing rights that are not being used can be leased to another person for 2 years maximum. The lease must be renewed at the end of the 2 years, even if nothing in the agreement has changed. *(Government Guidance on Managing Common Land, xvi)*

Local agreements

DEFRA and Natural England oversee the various levels of Stewardship Agreements that apply to farms and to commons. Commoners and landowners can set up a Commons Council to manage commons. Commons Councils are statutory groups: they are recognised by law, and can make legally binding rules for how people use the common land.

Commoners and landowners can also set up voluntary groups called Commons Associations, which usually have no legal power and rely on their members to agree about how the common should be managed. They can however sign legally binding agreements or guarantees about how members must treat the common, if all members agree. A joint agreement among graziers to put their common land into Higher Level Stewardship, for example, can over-ride previous or traditional arrangements and become enforceable in law.

Landowners

The largest landowners include the Lake District National Park Authority and United Utilities. Helvellyn, for example, is shared between the Lake District National Park Authority on the east side, and United Utilities on the west. Other owners in Cumbria include the National Trust; Natural England; the Ministry of Defence; the Royal Society for the Protection of Birds; and private estates such as Lowther.

Landowners may own, for instance, the mineral rights on the common, or the game shooting rights, without having any actual rights to put livestock onto the land. They are involved in making any agricultural agreements which affect the common. The landowner of a common can take action to stop anyone from exceeding their rights. *(Government Guidance on Managing Common Land, xvii)*

Natural England (NE) is an executive non-departmental public body, sponsored by DEFRA, and acts as the government's adviser for the natural environment in England. On any registered common land, or town or village greens with rights of common, NE can for instance stop someone:

- grazing livestock on land without the right to do so
- grazing a type of animal that they don't have permission or rights to graze
- exceeding their commons rights
- removing or cutting vegetation without legal authority. There are other unauthorised activities.

(Government Guidance on Managing Common Land, xviii)

Fell Pony Hill Breeders

The Fell Pony Society's definition of a Hill Breeder (2018) is recorded in Council Minutes: "The following definition was agreed. To have 'rights on common land to graze and be an active grazier.'" *(July 2018, xix)* There is no definition of how many ponies constitute "a herd."

It should be pointed out that the actual numbers of registered ponies are healthy *(Stud Book entries 2015 – 2021, xx)*.

Foals registered in the UK 2015-2021 *(Fell section of Grassroots database, xxi)*

	2015	2018	2021
Hillbred	82	97	126
Total UK	203	346	285
Total foals reg'd, Grassroots (excl. EU)	267	356	322
Hillbred as % of UK foals	40%	28%	44%
Hillbred as % of foals reg'd, Grassroots	31%	27%	39%

The 2019 list of hill herds included several new or revived prefixes (23 in total) but in 2021 two large studs, Bybeck and Greenholme, sold the majority of their stock. In 2021 these two had produced almost a third of all the foals born to hill herds. Whether the vacant common rights can be taken up by new breeders remains to be seen but for now, the number of foals being born to hill herds in 2022 will be significantly reduced.

A new herd?

Given all the preceding information, for anyone to establish a new fell-going herd of ponies now they must –

- either have enough money to buy and run property that has rights on common land,
- or be able to lease existing, unused grazing rights and to renew them on a 2-year basis.

The common rights would have to include a specific, or exchangeable, right to graze ponies. It depends entirely on the arrangements for a particular common, whether graziers can swap cattle or sheep rights for ponies. Long-term leasing depends on the continuing goodwill of the original rights-holder.

Rights to graze ponies on common land may still exist which are not being used. However, it will involve difficult and lengthy research just to find out where they are, let alone whether they have lapsed or what constraints or agreements are in place.

Other considerations

Examples

Grazing rights can be extinguished by commoners' agreements, eg on Crosby Ravensworth Fell the commoners decided in the 1980s to remove rights for horses and ponies. Rights can also be extinguished temporarily or permanently by landowner actions. In 2018 the Ministry of Defence applied to "de-register" its 4,500 hectares of common land (Murton, Hilton and Warcop Fells) near Warcop training area, having already bought-out the rights on adjacent areas in 2002 *(xxii)*. In 2022 Crosby Ravensworth Commoners Association intend to enter their fell into a Countryside Stewardship Agreement (CSA) which includes fencing and planting areas for scrub regrowth.

There may be unwanted side effects of new arrangements imposed on a common, even with the best of intentions. NE's acting area manager for Cumbria said in August 2019 (in a longer statement about common land management), "Natural England are supportive of Fell ponies as an important part of the cultural heritage of the area and for the conservation benefits they can bring through appropriate grazing. However, too many animals in the wrong place can damage upland habitats." *(xxiii)* This pressure on habitat may not necessarily be due to obvious overstocking in the sense of "too many animals for the total area of the common". Fenced areas or "exclosures" necessarily increase pressure elsewhere.

Other examples cropped up in conversations with hill breeders:

Walkers and trail-bike riders may disturb grazing livestock, whether they mean to or not, and that can discourage the animals (not just ponies) from using the full area of a common. Particularly where there are fenced-off sections, the stock can become heafed to a smaller area and the concentration may cause more damage to the ground than they would have done if they had been undisturbed.

Fenced areas may compel grazing animals to travel, for example between grazing and watering places, through a more constricted "funnel", causing eroded tracks and poaching. Also where new areas are fenced, they may create a barrier across the animals' normal routes to shelter in bad weather, which could be a welfare issue in a severe winter.

Winter feeding of animals may be restricted on a common to prevent spilled forage smothering low growing flora. In that case, feeding must be done elsewhere, eg on concrete "pads" near the farm. That, however, encourages the stock to move daily from their preferred grazing and sheltering areas back to the farm to feed, and the traffic again can cause erosion.

Implications for the Fell pony on the fells

The FPS – and the Fell Pony Breeders' Association (FPBA), which has members on FPS Council – have a major role in supporting the existence of the free roaming Fell pony herds. FPS Council is made up almost entirely of pony breeders, and six members of Council are hill breeders (in 2022: Bybeck, Greenholme [2], Lownthwaite, Townend, Wellbrow). FPS is in touch with Commoners' associations and Commoners' councils. A Society Council member attends meetings of the Federation of Cumbria Commoners. The FPS Secretary has to attend certain meetings with DEFRA and Natural England.

Although NE and DEFRA have an interest in the management of the commons, with the best will in the world they don't have enough staff to be in close contact with these huge areas of land every day. The people who have the most information on which to base decisions are the people who do see it and use it regularly, ie, the graziers and the Fell pony hill breeders. Some have already achieved reasonable agreements with regulatory bodies. If FPS can document and share what is working for them, including how to deal with civil problems such as public access and stock disturbance, they can advise people who need similar arrangements elsewhere.

Pony presence on hill commons depends on agreements and good relations between all the graziers on a common, as well as with Natural England. As one of my interviewees summed it up: "It's a shared fell, that's what 'common' means – you have to keep in with your neighbours!"

This article was originally published in the *FPS Magazine*, 2019, and *Native Pony Magazine*, 2020.

References are in a separate section at the end of the book, p216.

View from the Galloway Stone (foreground) across to the Shap Fells. Photo, Sue Millard

MAGNIFICENT MARES

Linnel

2249 Flora III f.1905

Flora III was a grey, with a "white face and both hind legs". Bred by the sporting "Yellow Earl" Lord Lonsdale, she was by the black stallion Mighty Atom 382 out of Polly II. At 13.1hh she was a very typical Fell height, her grey colour coming from her dam's line which went back to her great-grand-dam, a mare called Old Dunny who was of course dun but produced a grey filly when put to a grey called Telegraph. Telegraph was described in the pedigree of Tenison Pendragon 428 as "a half-bred Arab owned by Mr Bomfield-Soulby", and had been used a good deal in the district south of Penrith and Appleby; he was also behind the Peepings "Nancy Grey" line.

Grey seems to have been a popular colour of the time; Teesdale Comet was grey, as were Hilton Fashion (Hilton Passion) and Park End King, all stallions better known on the Dales side of the Pennines but present in Fell pedigrees. Perhaps Telegraph's stock were also notable for speed, which Lord Lonsdale prized; at any rate, after he sold Flora to Henry Holme of Thrimby, he bought back several fillies out of her - 2891 Ousel (f.1908), 2890 Swallow III (f.1909) and 2889 Hoopoe (f.1910), all by Dalesman. Ousel was piebald (more about her near the end of the book), Swallow was black with a grey patch on her nose, and Hoopoe was brown. In 1913 Flora foaled a black filly for Mr Holme, which was 2916 Flirt III (below, as a mature mare) and in 1917 3722 Fancy II, both again by Dalesman. Flora was obviously a "good nick" with Dalesman and he got fillies each time.

Flora III's 1913 daughter, 2916 Linnel Flirt, with her own filly foal 4894 Linnel Coquette by Guy Mannering (937 Dales). 1st prize winners at the Royal Agricultural Society of England Show (Newcastle) in 1923. Photo, Charlton Collection

110

At this point the story moves to The Linnels, in Northumberland, when Roy B Charlton bought Flora III's fillies Flirt III and Fancy II, whom he re-registered as 2916 Linnel Flirt and 3722 Linnel Fancy.

In 1925 Linnel Flirt was bred to Linnel Moor Boy 1441 and the following year produced 5624 Linnel Fluff; who in 1930 produced Linnel Gallant Boy 1704 (by Linnel Mite 1460, who was by Mountain Ranger). Linnel Fluff was later sold to King George V, who bought several ponies from the Charltons' stud including 5648

5896 Linnel Flora, daughter of L Coquette (opposite page) probably at Crook-a-beck, Patterdale, in the 1930s. Photo, Charlton Collection.

Linnel Wanda (p114) on whom he was photographed riding in London.

The Fell mares that the King bought in the 1930s formed the nucleus of the Windsor stud which was continued by King George VI, and sparked the interest of the Princesses Elizabeth and Margaret, who both drove a Fell in harness at Windsor Horse Show.

Her Majesty Queen Elizabeth II registered a Fell colt as Windsor Caravan 3309 in 1952, and the first Balmoral ponies in 1962. She became Patron of the Fell Pony Society in 1982.

Princess Elizabeth winning the harness class at Windsor Horse Show in 1945 with 7060 Windsor Gipsy (previously Railton Gipsy Black Princess, bred by Mrs Railton in Derbyshire) put to a Victoria pony phaeton. In 1944 Princess Margaret had won the class with the same pony to a governess car.
King George VI and Queen Elizabeth are spectating (front row, far right).
Gipsy was by Linnel Gallant Boy 1704 out of 6481 Dalemain Gipsy Queen (out of Robinson's Gipsy).
Photo, FPS archive in Cumbria Archive Centre, Kendal

Linnel Fluff's son Linnel Gallant Boy was the sire of the handsome Linnel Romany II 2400 (below). Romany II was chosen to run in the FPS Enclosure in 1948 and also sired some of the first Balmoral ponies.

Linnel Romany II 2400 f.1940, black, by L Gallant Boy out of 902 L Roma, about 1948 - NPS Show at Roehampton, with Billy Stephenson. L Romany II stood at The Nettles enclosure in 1945.

Photo, W Rouch & Co, from the Charlton Collection

Bob Charlton with 8575 Linnel Flighty f.1947, by Linnel Gipsy Lad 2630 out of 7421 Linnel Kathleen (by Linnel Gallant Boy 1704). Photo, Charlton Collection

Bob Charlton's favourite pony of all time was a mare called 8575 Linnel Flighty (by Linnel Gipsy Lad 2630, a grandson of 3775 Robinson's Gipsy who was by Glengarry 640, a sire line unrelated to that of Flora III). Flighty was very well known on the show circuit (opposite page and p178) and in the hunting field.

Bob said of Flighty: "She not only won lots of prizes, she was very rarely less than first. She hunted, she jumped, she was fun, she pulled, she was naughty, she bred some good foals, and yet anybody could ride her, as long as they could ride. I think she was probably – in my lifetime – the best."

The pairing of Flighty with Linnel Romany II produced Linnel Romany Boy 5257.

Despite his good-looking parents, Linnel Romany Boy was not a remarkably handsome pony and he was not often shown. His nickname at home was "Lord Little Ears" for his ability to slip-off a bridle or headcollar, even if sewn into his mane. He only attended the FPS Stallion Show once, at Lowther, where he disgraced himself by getting loose and leaving Bob Charlton holding a halter but no horse. He was recaptured, without any mischief, by the spectators who surrounded him and shepherded him into Bob's trailer. I saw this happen; it was the first Stallion Show I had ever attended and possibly the most amusing.

Linnel Romany Boy 5257 f.1968, seen here aged 23. Photo, Roy Wallis

This photo of Linnel Romany Boy always reminds me of Roy B Charlton's reaction when he saw Blooming Heather as an old stallion. But despite Linnel Romany Boy's ordinary appearance, he carried the lines of outstandingly good-looking and able ponies: Flora III and Mountain Ranger, Linnel Flighty, Linnel Romany II (and Linnel Gallant Boy twice). He passed the looks and ability on to his offspring with such success that for 3 consecutive years he won the Ponies of Britain Progeny Award as the sire of prize-winners - 2nd in 1975, and 1st in 1976, '77 and '78.

Linnel Romany Boy sired over 30 ponies at home at Linnel Wood including Linnel Mozart FP522G, Linnel Rapier II FP50212C, and Linnel Riddler FP50520C*. He also sired 13 ponies for Ailie Newall's Dene stud near Corbridge.

So we trace a long line of ponies, some ridden by a King or driven by a future Queen and her husband - and all descended from one 13.1 grey mare called Flora III.

King George V riding 5648 Linnel Wanda f.1927, accompanied (r) by Sir Arthur Erskine, 30 May 1932. Photo, Charlton collection

Linnel Rapier 2825 by Linnel Lingcropper 1621 out of 59020 Linnel Roma (daughter of 3775 Robinson's Gipsy). Photo, Charlton collection

HRH the Duke of Edinburgh arriving at Balmoral with the Balmoral dog-cart at the end of the Silver Jubilee Drive in 1977, with HM The Queen as his box-seat passenger, and Crown Equerry Sir John Miller standing behind. The Fell pony pair are 12601 Packway Swallow and her son Balmoral Martin G449 (by Balmoral Laddie 4424 who was by Linnel Romany II 2400.)

Photo, FPS Archives

HRH the Duke of Edinburgh in 1990 with a four in hand of Fells during the marathon phase of Lowther Driving Trials.

Photo, Roy Wallis

Waverhead

" MAYFLOWER-O'-THE-HILL." Three-year-old Filly
who took part in the pageant of horses and ponies at Harringay, 1951.

8787 Mayflower o'the Hill, Jim Bell's three-year-old filly who took part in the Native Pony pageant at Harringay, 1951. Photo, FPS Archives at Cumbria County Archive, Kendal

Jim Bell with 8649 Bank House Polly, f.1947, by Linnel Raven II 2631 out of 8247 Townend Polly II.

Photo, FPS Archives

Waverhead Blossom at Penrith Show 1963. Left to right, Barbara Bell, Jim Bell and Bim Tyson who is holding Waverhead Blossom (1st prize). W Molly was 2nd and W Jester 3rd in the same class. Bim Tyson used to drive the wagon for the Bells when they went to shows.
Photo, courtesy of the Bell family.

Jim Bell and his champion filly 13922 Waverhead Peggy f.1968, by Waverhead Rambler 4101 out of 12129 Townend Polly VIII, at the 1970 Breed Show. Photo, courtesy of the Bell family.

Mr. James Bell's Waverhead Peggy, overall champion at the Fell Pony Society
Breed Show at Penrith, with Mrs. Nancy Lightfoot. RIGHT: Lord Inglewood
takes up the reins of a racing sulkie during the Lowther Driving Trials.

Champion at the Breed Show, 13922 Waverhead Peggy, with Mrs Nancy Lightfoot.

12829 Waverhead Polly with her 1971 foal 14890 Waverhead Jewel, handled by Nancy Lightfoot.
Photo, courtesy of the Bell family.

13286 Waverhead Magic and FP1198* Redhouse Dusty
by Clive Richardson

Of the many champion Fell ponies bred by Jim Bell and his family, one of the most memorable was a black mare called Waverhead Magic, sired by Waverhead Rambler, and a mainstay of the Bells' show team for many years.

Waverhead Magic after winning the Supreme Mountain & Moorland Championship at Royal Windsor Show in 1976, shown by Barbara Bell. Photo courtesy of Hilary Lightfoot.

As well as contesting in-hand classes with great success, Magic was ridden by Barbara Bell in the show ring. Jim Bell drove Magic in the driving classes that were a feature of many agricultural shows at the time, usually harnessed to a dogcart that had once been owned by an Irish clergyman. When Horse Driving Trials were first introduced, Magic competed at the Lowther Castle Driving Trials four times.

However, it was not just Magic's many showing wins that made her exceptional, it was her versatility. At the Carlisle Jubilee Pageant in 1977, a historical re-enactment at the Castle that involved evening performances for a week and featured around ten Fell ponies, a horse-drawn litter bearing the "king" was carried by Magic and her stable-mate, Leithenwater Caraway. Despite a minimum of harness and the flimsy construction of the litter, both ponies performed admirably at every performance without mishap.

On another occasion Magic appeared in Ken Russell's 1978 TV film "Clouds of Glory," the story of William Wordsworth and his sister, Dorothy, which was shot at Dove Cottage, Grasmere, and starred Felicity Kendal.

Between the many shows and events she did over the years including carrying a bride to her wedding in the trap, Barbara's niece, Hilary Lightfoot, learnt to ride on Magic too.

Mr Jim Bell and Barbara-Bell with Waverhead Magic driving at Lowther

Jim Bell driving Waverhead Magic at Lowther Driving Trials in 1973.

Photo, FPS Magazine 2002

Carlisle Jubilee Pageant

Waverhead Magic (lead pony) and Leithenwater Caraway carry a litter at the
Carlisle Jubilee Pageant in 1977. Photo, FPS Newsletter

In later life Magic bred a number of foals including Waverhead Prince II, champion at the 2000 Fell Pony Society Stallion Show, and she was put down aged 24 after a brilliant show career which had done much to publicise the breed.

Magic's half-sister, the dark bay Redhouse Dusty, also by Waverhead Rambler, was another phenomenally successful pony, winning many ridden Fell classes over the ten years she was shown under saddle by Barbara before she was retired to stud. Dusty's progeny included the stallion, Waverhead Copper, as successful under saddle as he was at stud, and Waverhead Dusty who was used as a brood mare for several years before being brought back into work as a riding pony. In 2021 aged 26 Waverhead Dusty won the Veteran class at the Dorset County Show and also won the Veteran Pair class with one of Copper's offspring.

FP1198* Redhouse Dusty f.1982, was shown under saddle by either Barbara Bell (seen above) or Nancy Bell. Dusty was Champion ridden mare at the 1987 FPS Breed Show and many others. Dusty was by Waverhead Rambler out of 14589 Redhouse Mandy (B). Photo, FPS Archives

17142* Border Black Empress f.1975

Clive Richardson

Border Black Empress aged 4, Fell champion at the Ponies of Britain Show, Kelso, in 1979

Border Black Empress was by Jim Bell's champion stallion Waverhead Rambler 4101, out of 14210 Lunesdale Lady, a mare bred by Bert Morland *[by Heltondale Sonny Boy out of 12710 Sleddale Dainty III. Lady traced to Heltondale Romer 2540 five times in her pedigree, while Rambler traced twice to Storm Boy].*

Clive Richardson with Empress's dam, Lunesdale Lady. Photo courtesy of Michael Goddard.

Unshown until she was a two year old, Empress was loaned to Jim Bell for the 1977 show season and shown with success in youngstock classes. On the day her dam died at the Lowther Driving Trials of Blackleg (a clostridial disease usually associated with sheep) Empress won her first championship at Appleby Show and never looked back.

The following year Empress was shown in-hand at a number of local shows, winning a series of breed championships. That summer I quietly broke her to ride then hacked her out, often riding her over undulating broken ground at a walk on a loose rein to encourage her to use her head and neck to develop her natural balance. Brought out under saddle as a four year old, her many wins in 1979 included both the breed championship and the ridden class at

122

the Ponies of Britain Show, Kelso, as well as the ridden championship at the FPS Breed show, where she also qualified for the Mountain and Moorland Ridden Pony of the Year Final at Olympia, the first Fell to qualify as well as the youngest pony in the final.

In those days temporary stabling for Olympia was at a railway siding half a mile from the stadium, and the journey between them in the London traffic was fraught with danger. I decided I would have more control riding her, but passing a queue of people waiting for a bus she shied at heavy traffic and scattered them in all directions. I took her onto the pavement behind the re-assembled queue to pass them on the inside and she shied at her reflection in a plate glass shop window and scattered them in the other direction. In the show, despite her inexperience, she was placed fourth out of the 31 finalists and the ridden judge, Jennie Loriston-Clarke, commended her on her individual performance.

Over the winter when she was rising four I broke her to harness, beginning with her pulling a set of pony-sized chain harrows before putting her between the shafts of a breaking cart. After a challenging start, when she launched herself and the breaking cart into the air on more than one occasion, she settled down to work in harness and I showed her successfully in the driving class at the 1979 Breed Show harnessed to a gig. That year she also competed at the Holker Hall Driving Trials and won a class at the Northern Driving Championship Show.

In 1980 I took her to the Royal Show where she won the Fell championship on one of the wettest days in the show's history. Having been towed off the showground because of the ground conditions, there was then so much mud on the road that a convoy of tractors was needed to tow vehicles even on tarmac. Other notable wins that year included the reserve native championship at the Northern Counties Show, the reserve supreme championship at the FPS Breed Show, and the Ponies of Britain Show at Peterborough where she won the Fell championship, the class for Fells under saddle and the mixed Mountain and Moorland Working Hunter Pony class under three different judges.

In 1981 Empress was selected by the Fell Pony Society Council to represent the breed in the Knight, Frank & Rutley Knockout Stakes at the Royal Windsor Horse Show, a timed cone driving competition aimed to showcase the versatility of native breeds. Other driving successes included a number of private driving classes at agricultural shows, a couple of one day driving trials, and she was a runner-up in the Lanson Champagne Concours d'Elegance at the Lowther Horse Driving Trials.

Border Black Empress in 1979, FPS Archive

Like many Fell ponies, Empress was a competent jumper, placing second in the National Pony Society Mountain and Moorland Working Hunter Pony of The Year final at Malvern in 1984, and winning the Native Breeds handy pony class at the NPS show another year. She won the Fell Pony Performance Trials at Rydal on at least one occasion, plus the Performance Trials held at Packway, the home of former FPS secretary Peggy Crossland, three times in succession.

Overall, her many wins included the ridden championship at the FPS Breed Show on four occasions, the points trophy at the same show three times, and innumerable in-hand championships including winning three breed championships on three consecutive days.

Retired to stud, she proved equally successful as a brood mare. She produced nine foals in total including:

• Border Black Lady, (above) champion at the Royal Show in 1992 and female champion and reserve supreme champion at the 1994 Breed Show;

• Border Rambling Rose, a prolific winner in-hand and under saddle who also bred the youngstock champion at the 2007 Breed Show;

• and Border Duchess, another consistent prize winner.

One of Empress's colt foals, Border Black Prince II, was sold to Holland as a stallion. Another, Border Rambler, went to a breeder in Germany, while a third colt, Border Black Prince, stood at stud in Dorset and his many progeny (59 registered) included the Fell champion at the Royal Cornwall Show.

HM The Queen sent several of her mares to Border Black Prince and produced a number of prize-winning ponies with her Balmoral prefix including Balmoral Royalty and Balmoral Buckler, full brothers who were first and second in the novice working hunter pony class at the 2019 Breed Show and second and third in the preliminary dressage class at the Southern Breed Show. Another Black Prince son, Balmoral Phantom, driven by The Queen's granddaughter, Lady Louise Windsor, won the class for young drivers at the British Driving Society championships, while another son was a member of The Queen's Fell pony four-in-hand driven by HRH The Duke of Edinburgh.

Empress was put down in 2007 at the age of 32.

Heltondale

The Heltondale name crops up throughout the book, particularly with respect to Htd Black Prince III; indeed a whole book might be devoted to the mares from the Nobles' Heltondale stud - as it might be to those of Townend, Waverhead, Tebay, Murthwaite, Lunesdale and Wellbrow. Sarge and his brother Thomas farmed 100 acres at Butterwick, Bampton, but they also had grazing rights for cattle, sheep and ponies over the fell commons from Askham and Bampton to Haweswater and Sleddale, Ullswater and Kentmere. This enabled them, like some of the other well-known prefixes, to produce and support large numbers of ponies and thus be highly influential in the shaping of the breed.

Many Heltondale ponies are mentioned throughout this book, but I will have to keep this short to leave some space for the rest.

Heltondale-bred ponies ready to set off on a trek, summer 1962. Photo, Mrs Greta Noble.

Here is a small sample, starting with **8187 Lady Ann III, f.1940**. Owned and bred by Thomas Noble, who was then living at Keld Head, Heltondale, this mare was sired by Swinburn Boy 2364. Swinburn Boy was by Jock of Highwinder, whose pedigree is unrecorded, but Lady Ann's dam was Lady of Heltondale who was by Heltondale Victor 938, and through him she traces back to Comet II.

Lady Ann III was the dam of 11521 Lady II of Heltondale who had 4 foals, and 11937 Heltondale Polly Perkins who had 2 foals in the ownership of Walter Lloyd at Hades Hill.

I have not found a photograph of Lady Ann III, but she also produced 12833 Heltondale Rose who had 9 foals and 34 descendants, and they included the tiny but prolific **15024 Heltondale Rose V** whose story, documented by Liz Whitley, follows here.

15024 Heltondale Rose V f. 1969
Liz Whitley

Heltondale Rose V was foaled in 1969 and was out of the bay mare 12833 Heltondale Rose, who, in turn, was out of 8187 Lady Anne III, immediately taking us back to 1940. Rose V was by Heltondale Ranger 4778, who was by H. Mountain Prince 4184 (by 3751 Heltondale Prince). She was the prettiest pony I have ever known.

I can still remember the day that Rose arrived in Leicestershire in 1973, in foal to Heltondale Black Jock. She produced a colt foal, Wolds Dunlin. She was not put back to the stallion and the following year went away to be broken, but she is the only pony I have ever

Htd Rose V and family, around 1994: L to R, Wolds Lapwing, Jane Glass, Wolds Redstart, Heltondale Rose V (yes, she was only 12.2hh), Wolds Songthrush, Laura Sanders, and Wolds Woodcock. Photo, Liz Whitley

known who was impossible to break to ride. Not out of nastiness but out of terror. She was absolutely terrified of hands and so I learned the first lesson with wild ponies. Don't wave your hands about, if possible put them in your pockets. Since then I have read that the best way to observe any wildlife is with your hands in your pockets.

After that failure, she came home and became a brood mare. And what a mare: 17 foals altogether. Given that her dam had 16 it is a fair tally between them. Jane Glass's stallion at that time was Waverhead Rob and the combination of those two bred some amazing foals.

Waverhead Rob 4649

Rob was by Jim Bell's famous stallion, Waverhead Rambler.

Rose's first foal was Wolds Redstart and like all of Rose's foals she was bay (some were more brown than bay in fact). Starty had a challenging start to life getting a fencing stake in her neck as a foal, which left a scar, but despite this she had a successful showing career in hand and under saddle and was a brilliant driving pony. She also bred both pure bred and out bred foals (to thoroughbreds).

In 1976 Rose foaled a colt, W. Red Grouse. He had an interesting life and became a canal pony, pulling a horse drawn narrow boat at Foxton Locks in Leicestershire. Jane did a stallion swap with Mr Swift of Bannisdale in 1977 and Charlie Drake came south whilst Rob went up to Cumbria. 1978 saw another colt foal, this time by Charlie Drake, W. Kingfisher, about whom I know little, although he was a lovely bay pony again.

One of Rose's most famous offspring, W. Goldfinch, was foaled in 1979. Finch had a fantastic ridden career and went on to win the Northlight Championship and had a model made of him, which proved very popular. Golden Eagle was the next Rose foal in 1980 and he too had a good showing career. He was followed by Kittiwake in 1981 and Golden Plover in 1983. Sadly, Plover died when quite young.

1984 saw W. Lapwing arrive and she, like several of Rose's foals, had a very long life reaching 32 or 33 I believe. She went up to Shetland for a period before coming back to Leicestershire where she taught many young people how to ride, hang on, swim a pony and so on. I hunted her a few times and usually stayed near the front, otherwise my arms grew an inch or two! Lapwing was the last Rose/Charlie Drake foal as Rob came home that year. She was brown although bay brown in summer.

Jack Snipe was the next foal 1985, by Rob this time. Despite Rose being 12.2 if she stood on tip toes, and Rob being 13.1, Snipe grew... and grew... to 14.2. The next Rose/Rob foal was Dabchick, who went north but was successful and we saw her at the breed show a few times.

In 1988 Songthrush arrived on the scene, not at the normal foaling time of the year, but on 30th September. She will be 34 this year (2022). I had decided, before she was even born, that if she was a filly I was going to buy her as she could be the last filly Rose had. She, like all of Rose's foals, has done everything from happy hacker to Le Trec, cross country, endurance, dressage and showing. One thing she has never done is hunt as she was a very excitable youngster and I felt it would blow her mind. She was very good at displaying her tummy to anybody, including judges, and wasn't averse to doing that with me on top. However, I never fell from her and I believe she was really quite safe. At 33 we still poddle round the Cornish lanes but once we trot her heritage comes to the fore and she just has to be in

Wolds Songthrush

front. I haven't mentioned that I traced her pedigree in the Rose line, back to Old Grey Shales, one of the fastest trotters in the country!

1990 saw the arrival, again in September, of the well-known Wolds Woodcock. Sadly, his life was too short (16), but he was the most amazing pony having great success in hand, under saddle, jumping, side saddle and dressage. I hunted him as a youngster and he was stunning and later in life he hunted regularly. I might add that our local hunt was the Quorn so we had exciting country and caused a few to wonder at our wonderful breed. He won the ridden championships at Lowther, Ponies UK, FPS Southern and many more. He is still sadly missed.

Woodie, Songthrush and Dabchick won the mare progeny class at the breed show and another year Rose's progeny again won the class, I think with Redstart, Songthrush and Woodcock but I can't be quite sure now.

Waverhead Rob died with liver disease in 1990 or 91 and Jane then stood Ralfland Victor. I'm unsure now as to whether the next two ponies are still alive, Curlew (1992) and Plover (1993).

Wolds Woodcock FP738G, f.1990. Taking part in the Fell show classes at Lowther. Photo, Laura Hart

Curlew went to Mrs Elisabeth Marshall and had a successful career.

I have checked the Grassroots database but I know it is not correct as it lists several of Rose's foals, that I know are dead, as still living.

128

FP50348C	Wolds Goldeneye	M	02 May 1995
FP50140C	Wolds Plover	M	22 Jun 1993
FP2169	Wolds Curlew	F	12 May 1992
FP738G	Wolds Woodcock	C	10 Sep 1990
FP1678	Wolds Songthrush	F	30 Sep 1988
FP324G	Wolds Jack Snipe	C	01 May 1985
FP1391	Wolds Lapwing	F	05 Jun 1984
7038	Wolds Golden Eagle	F	29 Jun 1980
16747	Wolds Redstart	F	

Sadly, Rose's last foal in 1995 had an accident as a foal and didn't survive. Rose herself became ill in 1996 and was put to sleep.

Heltondale Rose V was the most gentle mare and everyone loved her. For me, I'm glad that she couldn't be broken as she may have gone elsewhere and we would not have seen all these lovely ponies. Her progeny have touched the lives of so many people and I am sure that some of you reading this will have your own memories of one or more of them.

Thank you Sarge Noble for that wonderful little mare and thank you Jane Glass for letting me be part of her story.

Shilstone Rocks Blackberry and foal Wolds Osprey by Waverhead Rob. Photo, Liz Whitley

Townend & Carrock

14355 Townend Heather f.1970

Eddie Wilson with 14355 Townend Heather. Foaled in 1970, by Guards Hero III 4742 out of 10550 Roundthwaite Bell Heather, she won the Horse & Hound Cup at the Breed Show in 1973 and many other championships including the Royal Show. Photo courtesy of Penny Randell.

Townend Heather won the 'Horse & Hound' Native Pony Cup in 1973 as a 3 year old at the FPS Breed Show, a cup that went to a different native breed each season. She was the dam of 16 foals, which included: Townend Bramble II, Townend Hamish and Townend Hamish II; and grand-dam of Townend Biggles – all of which successfully competed at Olympia and Horse of the Year Show.

Heather was the dam of 16547 Townend Holly, f.1975, by Townend Flash II. Holly was very successful at local Cumbrian Shows.

Townend Holly and Penny Randell at Hesket Show, possibly 1984.
Photo courtesy of Penny Randell.

Photo of Mr and Mrs Eddie Wilson with 16635* Robbswater Ruth, and 16547 Townend Holly and Townend Holly II as a foal. Probably taken in 1976. Photo courtesy of Penny Randell

Eddie Wilson with 16635* Robbswater Ruth f.1975. By Townend Flash II 5278 out of 13119 Waverhead Julie. Champion at many local shows and at The Royal Show in 1985. Ruth bred 12 foals, which included the Townend Ruths, eg Townend Ruth IV. Also dam of Townend Robbie who was a successful stallion in Holland and Denmark. Photo courtesy of Penny Randell

FP2609 Townend Bethany f.1994. By Heltondale Josh FP587C* out of FP1683* Townend Bryony. Champion M & M at The Royal Highland Show in 2007 and Champion Mare at the Breed Show. Photo courtesy of Penny Randell.

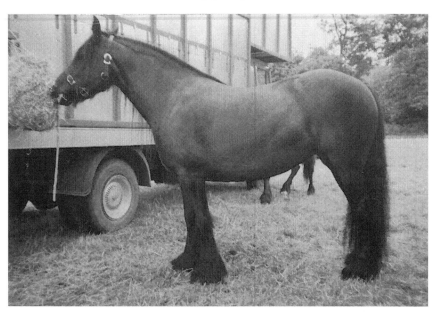

A Grand-dam of Skylark (opposite top) - 1988 Breed Show champion and Youngstock Champion, FP1551 Htd Maydew VII f.1986, by Black Prince FP188C* out of 16702 Heltondale May Dew. Photo, Joanne Exley.

FP5315 Townend Skylark f.2010, by Htd Bonzo Boy FP5011C* out of FP4025 Townend Sky.
Skylark was Supreme Champion at the 2018 breed show, exhibited by Jamie Cockbain. Another
example of a lovely pony resulting from a combination of IItd Black Prince, TC Victor and Lunesdale
Jerry lines. Photo, FPS Magazine (Claire Simpson).
Below and left, two of Skylark's grandparents.

A grandsire of Skylark (above) - Castle Hill Bellman FP51137C* by Htd Bellman V FP50289C* out of
FP2372 Htd Princess. Seen here happy and muddy at home, with Margaret Wilson. Photo courtesy of
Penny Randell.

FP2897* Townend Sugar f.1996
John Cockbain (Sugar's owner since 2004)

Sugar was bred by my late grandfather Eddie Wilson and his wife Margaret in 1996, by Drybarrows Jeff FP50048C*out of FP1515 Townend Shula. As I sit down to write about her it's hard to know where to start as she has meant so much in so many different ways to us all. She has been successful in the show ring, very successful at breeding quality offspring, helped various family members learn to ride and show in hand and has just generally been a real character and member of the family.

*FP2897*Townend Sugar with Imogen and Connor Cockbain*

Sugar spent the first 5 years of her life at Townend before being given to my mother Glenis in late 2001. The following year we took Sugar and her foal Carrock I'm Yer Man to our local show at Keswick. The late Chris Thompson of Drybarrows Stud was the judge and he had some strong classes in front of him that day. Sugar won the mare class shown by my brother James Cockbain, and I showed I'm Yer Man who won the foal class. Sugar went on to take the Championship honours.

We were delighted on the day but as time passed the wins took on more significance as that was the last Keswick show Eddie Wilson would be alive for. It was wonderful that one of his own, shown by his family, would take the top honours at our local show. It was also fitting that Chris Thompson would give out top honours to both Sugar and in particular I'm Yer Man who has in recent years been breeding at Drybarrows with much success.

FP6278 Carrock Lilly by Boutime Wooster FP71820C* out of FP2897 Townend Sugar.
Foal & Youngstock show champion 2018, with John Cockbain.

FP6003 Carrock Elsa f.2014 (grey) by Murthwaite Timothy FP70695C* out of FP2897 Townend
Sugar, with John, Imogen and Connor Cockbain

Sugar has been a real foundation for breeding Carrock ponies. She has won the best mare performance points award on a number of occasions thanks to her successful offspring. 6 of them have won classes on at least one occasion at the FPS breed show and I'm Yer Man has won the stallion show championship numerous times. Since the North West Area Support Group's foal show expanded to include youngstock in 2014, Sugar has been either the dam or grand dam of the winner: in 2015 (Carrock Elsa), 2016 (Drybarrows Another Chapter), 2018 (Carrock Lilly) and 2021 (Carrock Duke was foal and supreme champion, and Carrock Daenerys was youngstock champion).

Not many ponies get the chance to be involved with so many generations of one family but Sugar has played her part in four generations of ours. She has had a special connection with all of us. Tracey is convinced that in spring 2008 Sugar kept gently nudging her around her tummy because she knew before we did that our daughter Imogen was in there.

Townend Sugar being successfully shown by Imogen Cockbain. Photo, Lucy Jones

As many of you will know Fell ponies can have a real stubborn streak and Sugar is no exception. Plenty of photos over the years have either taken far longer than necessary or have been spoiled by Sugar sulking. That said, when it really matters Sugar has always been there for our family. She helped teach my wife Tracey to ride and helped both my son and daughter to do the same.

Sugar was the go-to pony to introduce Imogen to the show ring and always showed the right amount of patience balanced with enough spark to show a 7 year old girl what to do.

In 2016 as a 20 year old mare Sugar (shown by Imogen) won the championship at Hesket-new-market show. Some of you will know this is the local show for the Townend stud so it was quite fitting that Sugar won it with her breeder's great granddaughter showing her.

Sugar is still going strong at 25 and fingers crossed should hopefully give us another foal next spring. She is very much part of our present and future with three of her current offspring here at Rakefoot at the moment, and also a big part of our past.

One of the most influential ponies in mother's life (Glenis Cockbain) was the legendary Townend Flash II who is Sugar's grand sire. Flash holds the astonishing honour of winning the FPS stallion show a record 9 times! Flash was in the bloodlines of Carrock Pollyanna, the first homebred filly of the Carrock Fells and one of the most successful. I would like to think Flash's quality plays its part in Sugar's consistent breeding over the years.

We feel Sugar has really left her mark both with us at the Carrock stud and in the breed and we look forward to as many more years as possible with her.

Carrock I'm Yer Man FP51327C*, Supreme Champion, 2007 Stallion & Colt Show, Dalemain, owned and exhibited by Alistair Smith, Bracklinn Stud. I'm Yer Man is out of Townend Sugar by Castle Hill Jerry FP50855G*. Photo, FPS Photo Gallery

Champion at the Foal Show 2021, Carrock Duke FP73396G.
Photos, Claire Simpson/Cockbain family

Sleddale

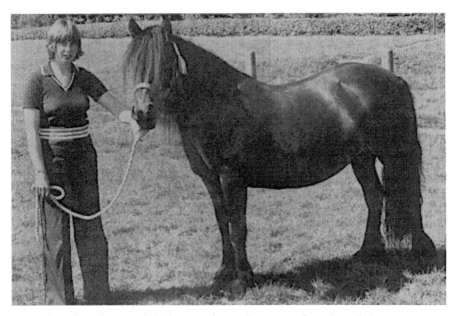

Pat Alexander with 16313 Sleddale Rose X f.1974, champion at the FPS Breed Show in 1979. By Sleddale King of the Fell 5902 out of 14631 Sleddale Rose VII, by Heltondale Sonny Boy 4475. Photo, FPS Magazine archives

The Sleddale herd came into being in the 19th century when Joseph Harrison farmed at Sleddale Hall. The ponies were used on the farm for shepherding. A love for the ponies continued through Joseph's son John William, and then through Henry farming at Thorny Bank.

Just like the Dargue family (Peepings) and the Wales/Morton family (Lownthwaite), when I interviewed Henry Harrison for *Hoofprints in Eden* he could not pinpoint the origin of his ponies:

> Well, my grandfather had them like. Oldest certificate I have is dated 1932. I can't tell you before that, but I know my grandfather had them. Now and then, we had quite a lot; most we had ever was about forty I think. But not then, earlier days, they hadn't that many.

The Sleddale ponies were predominantly brown and notable for consistent pony type and hardiness. They ran out on Ralfland Common and over into Swindale grazing land up to 1400 feet. Henry Harrison's family were very involved in exhibiting their mares and young stock, especially at the Fell Pony Breed Show, the Sleddale Rose line being particularly successful.

Sleddale mares on the fell, Ralfland/Keld, Shap. Photos, Shap Local History Society (copies of pictures provided by Joyce Harrison, Thorny Bank, Sleddale)

Sleddale King of the Fell 5902, f.1969, by Heltondale Sonny Boy 4475, out of 13164 Sleddale Dainty V. Seen here at home at Thorny Bank, Shap.

Sleddale King of the Fell 5902 was a well-known stallion in the 1970s. Like Lunesdale Jerry, King of the Fell was not shown, but he had 56 offspring, and fillies by him won the progeny group class at the Breed Show 4 times between 1979 and 1984. The photograph above is courtesy of Ruth Eastwood, and believed to have been taken by Harry Tunstall of Foggy Gill, Fell End, Kirkby Stephen, who used King of the Fell on his grey mare 17759 Peggy of Foggy Gill who produced Foggy Gill Dapper (see *Mare Miscellany* section).

The stallion (bottom right) with mares at Sleddale may be King of the Fell but this is unconfirmed. He could equally well be Heltondale Sonny Boy or Lunesdale Richard. Photo, Shap Local History Society (copies of pictures provided by Joyce Harrison, Thorny Bank, Sleddale)

H H Postma's Sleddale Eddie FP50762C* (left) by Murthwaite Victor FP652G* out of FP1003 Sleddale Lib, and his son Odin van het Westerkwartier out of 200100137 Flora, prizewinners in Holland. Photo, courtesy of Joke Postma

Lt. Col. Sir John Miller presenting the Supreme Championship at the 1991 Fell Pony Society Southern Show, Horspath, nr. Oxford. The Champion was FP1117 Sleddale Beauty XXVII f.1981, by Lunesdale Jerry out of 16744 - Sleddale Beauty XXII, owned by Mr & Mrs Norton of Kent, bred by Mr T. H. Harrison, Shap. Photo, FPS Magazine archive.

Roundthwaite Lucky Jim 3258 f.1951

SHOW SPOTLIGHT

THERE was a disappointingly small entry of young stock at the **Fell Pony Society's** annual colt and stallion show at Penrith in May, due to the fact that fillies have been far more numerous than colts in recent foalings, but those that came forward were of excellent quality. Mr. R. Little had quite a field day, taking first prizes in all three classes and gaining the Lady Yule championship trophy with his four-year-old, Guards Hero II, whose sire, Guards Hero, won the same award in 1954 and was afterwards exported to Pakistan. The new champion was selected to stand at the Society's principal breeding enclosure at Berrier, and Miss P. Crossland's Packway Royal will be at the smaller enclosure at High Arnside.

The reserve champion was Mrs. G. F. S. Newall's Roundthwaite Lucky Jim, who had led the breed at the Ponies of Britain Club's spring stallion show and has been a prolific prize-winner, in hand and under saddle. After a somewhat chilly beginning.

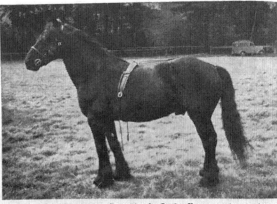

Mrs. Newall's Fell stallion, Roundthwaite Lucky Jim, a consistent winner.

"There was a disappointingly small entry of young stock at the Fell Pony Society's annual colt and stallion show at Penrith in May [1959], due to the fact that fillies have been far more numerous than colts in recent foalings, but those that came forward were of excellent quality..."

Reserve Champion was Roundthwaite Lucky Jim (by Storm Boy 2288 out of 8319 Syble).

Heltondale breeder Sarge Noble in 1978 at High House, Butterwick, riding 14156 Linnel Clare, who was sired by 3258 Roundthwaite Lucky Jim 3258 out of 13815 Linnel Caroline. June 1978.

Photo, Mrs Greta Noble.

Lunesdale

Bert Morland's Lunesdale Jerry 6841 f.1972, by Mountain Flash II 4745 out of 12710 Sleddale Dainty III. Jerry had 169 offspring, and his progeny won the group class at the Breed Show 5 times between 1982 and 1989. Photo courtesy of Carole Morland. Jerry's progeny won the group class at the FPS breed show 5 times between 1982 and 1989. He was not shown himself because although he was nice-natured, he was never bitted, which is a requirement for stallions being shown in public. Photo courtesy of Carole Morland

Lunesdale Lucky Lady FP1327 f.1983, by Townend Flash II 5278 out of 17847 Lunesdale Grey Dawn, shown by Lizzie Briant. Lucky Lady was the first Fell to be NPS Champion Mountain and Moorland Pony at Olympia. She had qualified 5 years running and been Best of Breed there 4 times; reserve Champion in 1988, 4th in 1989, 4th in 1990, 8th in 1991 and Champion in 1992.

Lunesdale Henry and Lunesdale White Rose

Lunesdale Henry 6932 f.1978, at an open day at the Lunesdale stud at Roundthwaite. He was by Lunesdale Jerry 6841 out of 17781 Adamthwaite Sandra. Photo, FPS Magazine.

FP1871 Lunesdale White Rose f.1982, was by Lunesdale Jerry 6841 out of 17780 Adamthwaite Dawn. Here she is at the FPS Breed show in 1991, with her filly by Henry, 2026 Lunesdale Rebecca winning the foal class. Thomas Capstick's Foggy Gill Prim (far end of the line-up) had won the brood-mare class, with White Rose second.

In front of Prim, wearing the cap, is Eddie Wilson who, having retired from running-out his own Townend mares, had become the regular steward for the brood-mare class. Photo, Roy Wallis.

6932 - Lunesdale Henry

Parents	Grand Parents	Great Grand Parents	Great Great Grand Parents
Lunesdale Jerry 6841 Black	Mountain Flash II 4745 Grey Roan	Waverhead Rambler 4101	Black Grouse 3733 Black / Jenny O' The Hill 8887
		Mountain Heather 8511 Roan	Linnet Raven II 2631 / Mountain Gypsy 8241
	Sleddale Dainty III 12710	Adamthwaite Lucky Star 4067	Heltondale Prince 3751 Dk Brown / Stouphill Pride 10599
		Sleddale Dainty 11694	Merry John III 3709 / Sleddale Beauty III 10414
Adamthwaite Sandra II 17781	Heltondale Sonny Boy 4473 Black	Heltondale Star Boy 3854	Heltondale Prince 3751 Dk Brown / Gipsy Pearl 9264
		Fuesdale Black Bess of Heltondale 11658	Heltondale Romer 2540 / Dot of Keld Head 8321 Dk Brown
	Adamthwaite Sandra 12944	Heltondale Prince 3751 Dk Brown	Heltondale Romer 2540 / Blackbird VII 8165
		Sleddale Stella 17436	Borwick Warrior 3160 / Sleddale Rose III 9339

FP1871 - Lunesdale White Rose

Parents	Grand Parents	Great Grand Parents	Great Great Grand Parents
Lunesdale Jerry 6841 Black	Mountain Flash II 4745 Grey Roan	Waverhead Rambler 4101	Black Grouse 3733 Black / Jenny O' The Hill 8887
		Mountain Heather 8511 Roan	Linnet Raven II 2631 / Mountain Gypsy 8241
	Sleddale Dainty III 12710	Adamthwaite Lucky Star 4067	Heltondale Prince 3751 Dk Brown / Stouphill Pride 10599
		Sleddale Dainty 11694	Merry John III 3709 / Sleddale Beauty III 10414
Adamthwaite Dawn 17780	Mountain Flash II 4745 Grey Roan	Waverhead Rambler 4101	Black Grouse 3733 Black / Jenny O' The Hill 8887
		Mountain Heather 8511 Roan	Linnet Raven II 2631 / Mountain Gypsy 8241
	Heltondale Princess 12135	Heltondale Prince 3751 Dk Brown	Heltondale Romer 2540 / Blackbird VII 8185
		Heltondale Doll's Pride 11657	Heltondale Romer 2540 / Dolly of Heltondale 11061

Pedigrees of Lunesdale Henry and L White Rose, from the Grassroots database (copyright of the FPS)

"I spoke to a gentleman some time ago on the subject of line breeding. He had achieved considerable success with the breeding of Welsh Cobs, and was of the opinion that it was perfectly all right to do it provided there were no serious or similar faults in mare and stallion, and there was a good outcross on both sides. I came to the conclusion that for the first time since I started breeding, I had the two ponies most suitable for this experiment, ic Lunesdale Henry and Lunesdale White Rose." (Bert Morland, *A Lifetime in the Fells*, 1995)

The Henry x White Rose cross produced three colts and three fillies:

 1990 Lunesdale Mountain Mist 716C

 1991 FP2026 Lunesdale Rebecca

 1993 FP2325 Lunesdale Lizzie

 1994 FP2545 Lunesdale Gypsy Rose

 1997 Lunesdale Monarch FP50707C*

 1999 Lunesdale Danny Boy FP50925C*

1990 Lunesdale Mountain Mist 716C f.1990, by Lunesdale Henry 6932 out of FP1871 Lunesdale White Rose. Winner of the Stallions over 10 Years class at the 2002 stallion show.

Photo, FPS Photo gallery.

The Henry x White Rose family already has over 300 members. For example:

Lunesdale Mountain Mist had 103 progeny and was exported, after a long career in Cumbria, to the Goodshapes stud in the Czech Republic.

Lunesdale Rebecca produced 7 foals including 3 active stallions:

> **Lunesdale Black Caviar FP72264C*** (exported to USA where he has sired 19 foals for Mary-Jean Gould-Earley's Laurelhighland stud;
>
> **Lunesdale Beckham FP51312C*** who has 80 progeny, mainly for Craig Mallinson's Midtown stud;
>
> **Lunesdale Union Jack FP72091C*** (32 progeny) who is still with Bert Morland's Lunesdale stud.

Rebecca's fillies include **FP3455 Lunesdale Lady Rebecca.**

Lady Rebecca had 9 foals, including **L Warlord FP71091C*** (right) who has sired 49 foals.

Lunesdale Warlord. Photo, Ruth Eastwood

LUNESDALE REBECCA   BREED SHOW SUPREME CHAMPION

FP2026 Lunesdale Rebecca f.1991, by Lunesdale Henry 6932 out of FP1871 Lunesdale White Rose. Breed Show champion in 2000 with Bert Morland. Photo by Fane Murray, in FPS Magazine.

"I know the Bible says 'thou shalt not covet', but I have to admit that I coveted ... Heltondale Princess. I begged Ted [Benson] to sell her to me on many occasions but he always refused. She epitomized all the good points as laid down by the Fell Pony Society and which Ted had always preached to me. She had good feet, joints and feather, marvellous flat bone and hocks, a beautiful head with small pointed ears and large nostrils, a well laid shoulder, good neck and short back." (Bert Morland, *A Lifetime in the Fells.*)

"First pony I had was Heltondale Princess. She was brown. I think she was just about best mare I ever had. I don't think she was as good as that mare of Bert's now, Rebecca, that mare he shows. There wouldn't be a lot of difference, but I think taking them all round Rebecca would be a better pony than Princess." (Ted Benson in 2004, for *Hoofprints in Eden*)

Given these remarks, Bert's own comment on Rebecca is interesting. He does not run through her show achievements but remembers Sarge Noble saying he had never seen a pony that good in his lifetime. "I thought that was the best compliment she could have had."

Sarge offered Bert a large sum of money for Rebecca. He turned it down.

Dene and Bewcastle

8644 Dene Black Beauty f. 1947

Dene Black Beauty was bred in Northumberland by Gerald FS Newall, by Linnel Gypsy Lad 2630 out of Linnel Blackbird 8081.

Beauty's daughter, 11928 Dene Beauty Belle f. 1958, was by Mrs Ailie Newall's well-known stallion Roundthwaite Lucky Jim 3258 (opposite page). In the show ring the Dene ponies were always beautifully turned out, well-schooled and fit, and they were instantly recognisable - see Dene Fire Flare, opposite page.

Dene Beauty Belle was bought by Mary Longsdon who founded her stud under the Bewcastle prefix, and Beauty Belle carried on the legacy of her mother Black Beauty.

DENE BLACK BEAUTY. Owned and bred by Mrs. G. F. S. Newall.

8644 Dene Black Beauty f. 1947 by Linnel Gypsy Lad 2630 out of 8081 Linnel Blackbird

Roundthwaite Lucky Jim, Fell Champion, Royal Show, 1956

Roundthwaite Lucky Jim 3258, Fell Champion at the Royal Show in 1956

Mrs Newall's 12378 Dene Fire Flare, by Roundthwaite Lucky Jim 3258 out of 7419 Dene Firefly
(Formerly Linnel Firefly) by Linnel Lingcropper 1621 x 6671 Linnel Firespark.
Fire Flare descended, through Linnel Lingcropper, from Flora III. Photo, Roy Wallis

Miss M Longsdon with 11928 Dene Beauty Belle f. 1958 by Roundthwaite Lucky Jim 3258 out of Dene Black Beauty; and Belle's 1969 foal Bewcastle Beacon 5246 by Waverhead Rob 4649

16844 Bewcastle Bonny f. 1976, at NPS Show. She was by Waverhead Rob 4649 out of 11928 Dene Beauty Belle. Photo, Richard & Carol Gilson.

Bewcastle Beacon 5246, 14448 Bouquet and 16844 Bonny
(all by Waverhead Rob out of Beauty Belle)

Michael Goddard with Bewcastle Boy Blue FP650G, f. 1989, by FP234C Waverhead Prince II out of
Bewcastle Bonny. Photo, Anthony Reynolds.

FP1523 Bewcastle Bella, f. 1986 by Waverhead Henry FP137C out of 16561 Bewcastle Beckstone (Waverhead Rob x Dene Beauty Belle).

FP3353 Bewcastle Blinky Bonny, f. 1999 by Waverhead Storm Boy III FP50574G* out of Bewcastle Bella (above). Bred by Mary Longsdon & Richard Goddard. Champion at NPS summer show, with sponsor Sheila Peet and judge Mrs Stella Hore, and owner Michael Goddard. Photo, Anthony Reynolds.

Michael Goddard with FP4092 Bewcastle Blossom, f.2004, by Border Black Prince FP454C* out of FP3353 Bewcastle Blinky Bonny. Bred by Mr M & R Goddard. Photo, 2013, JP Event Photography.

Grand-daughters of Beauty bred by Miss Longsdon out of Beauty Belle included 16561 Bewcastle Beckstone f.1975 and 16844 Bewcastle Bonny f.1976, both by Waverhead Rob 4649.

Bewcastle Beckstone produced FP1523 Bewcastle Bella f.1986 (photo opposite, top) by Waverhead Henry FP137C, and Bella in turn produced FP3353 Bewcastle Blinky Bonny f.1999 (photo opposite) by FP50574G* Waverhead Storm Boy III.

Blinky Bonny produced a filly (photo above): Bewcastle Blossom FP4092 f.2004 by FP454C* Border Black Prince. Blossom is not only a descendant of Dene Black Beauty, but through her sire she is also a grand-daughter of Border Black Empress (see chapter on Waverhead).

Photographs provided by: FPS Archives, the late Mary Longsdon, Michael Goddard

SUE MILLARD

Rackwood

Eileen Walker

My father, George Robert Coatsworth of East Rackwood Hill, Hamsterley near Bishop Auckland in County Durham, bought his first Fell pony in the spring of 1974. He had always been involved with horses and ponies through his work as a farmer and a father of five children who always had a pony to ride. This Fell pony was called Heltondale Dewdrop IV and was a two year old filly bred by the late Sarge Noble. My father registered the prefix "Rackwood" after the name of our home farm so that he could register Heltondale Dewdrop's offspring. In 1977 he registered Rackwood Queen followed in 1978 by Rackwood Dewdrop.

Queen and Dewdrop were handled and shown in-hand as youngsters and then broken to ride. They were regularly used to shepherd the sheep before becoming brood mares. Queen was sold in the autumn of 1989 but Dewdrop, who was a heavier and slightly taller pony, was kept and became a very successful brood mare.

Dewdrop was my father's favourite Fell pony. She matured at 13.1hh and had excellent feet and legs. She was a forward going pony who was a pleasure to ride and demonstrated true Fell pony movement when shown in-hand or ridden. During 1986 she won her first red rosettes competing in both in-hand and ridden classes. During the years that followed she was awarded Champion Fell pony on numerous occasions. She excelled as a broodmare and always produced a quality foal regardless of which stallion she was covered by. When she was newly foaled my father was the only person who could catch her, so when he took ill during the 1990s I had to wear his wax jacket and trilby hat in order to get close to her and I had to

18034 Rackwood Dewdrop by Frizington White Heather 4209 out of 15390 Heltondale Dewdrop IV (by Heltondale Heather Lad 5493). Dewdrop's foal is FP3487* Rackwood Maydew f.2000, by Heltondale Bonzo Boy FP50115C*.*

154

keep my face tilted down and not speak if I was to stand any chance of putting a rope halter over her ears. A real character who was head of the Rackwood herd for many years.

FP1366 Rackwood Velvet f.1984

Mr GR Coatsworth with FP1366 Rackwood Velvet, f.1984, champion as a 2-year-old at the FPS Breed Show 1986. Velvet was by Rambler of Ayresome 6728 out of 18034* Rackwood Dewdrop.

Rackwood Velvet was the first filly foal out of my father's favourite mare Rackwood Dewdrop. Velvet's gentle, kind and patient nature made her a pleasure to handle and I enjoyed breaking her to ride and hacking out around Hamsterley Forest. She was very successful in the show ring being FPS Breed Show Female Champion and Supreme Champion in 1986 and FPS Breed Show Female Champion in 1987. She was awarded Fell Pony Champion at many local shows throughout her life.

Rackwood Velvet in 2007, aged 23

155

My most memorable moment with Velvet was in 1987 when she won the Fell Pony Championship at Lowther Horse Driving Trials and Prince Philip came into the main ring to present the rosettes. Our lap of honour was overwhelming. When the spectators sitting on the embankment applauded I was lifted off the ground by Velvet as she went round the arena in an extended trot.

The current Rackwood herd are all descendants of Rackwood Dewdrop. I have never bought a female pony so I currently have five generations of Rackwood breeding.

FP3487* Rackwood Maydew f.2000

Dam: 18034* Rackwood Dewdrop, Sire: Heltondale Bonzo Boy FP50115C*

Maydew was a very sensible and solid type of pony. She was handled and shown as a foal with her mother, Rackwood Dewdrop, but then had to take a back seat to allow Magic to take centre stage. I broke her to ride in 2004 and continued to ride her throughout 2005. She was shown at local venues and was awarded Champion and Reserve Champion status on more than one occasion. She had a good length of stride and a powerful trot making her a pleasure to ride. She was used as a broodmare since 2006 and produced 14 healthy foals – 7 fillies and 7 colts. I have kept 3 fillies (Melody, Maggie May & Autumn Dew) but all of the colts have been sold. She was shown as a broodmare during the summer of 2018 and awarded several prizes including Reserve Champion at Eggleston Show.

Maydew died 18-09-2019, twelve days after giving birth to her 14th foal.

FP3487 Rackwood Maydew and her 2016 foal FP72611C* Rackwood Windsor, who was named for the Fell Pony Society's trip to Windsor that year with 135 Fell ponies to form a Guard of Honour for HM The Queen in celebration of her 90th birthday.*

Rackwood Magic f.2000

Dam: FP1881Rackwood Dawn, Sire: Heltondale Bonzo Boy FP50115C*

Magic is probably the most famous of my ponies. She was not handled as a foal because of my ill health nor shown as a yearling because of the Foot and Mouth restrictions but gained immediate show ring success when shown as a two year old and became FPS Breed Show Female Champion in 2003. I broke her to ride during the summer of 2003 but because of my work commitments decided to breed from her. Since 2004 she has been used as a broodmare and has produced 13 healthy foals – 7 fillies and 6 colts. As a broodmare Magic became FPS Breed Show Female Champion and FPS Breed Show Supreme Champion in 2007 (photo below).

She has been an excellent broodmare and mother and has produced some quality foals but in 2013 I thought she should have a change of career and become a ridden pony. That idea was very short lived because I have far too many ponies to ride so when Magic took a fancy to my new stallion, Linnel Riddler, she was soon back doing what she is good at, being a broodmare.

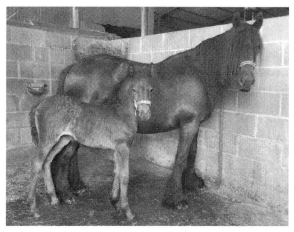

Magic and FP6686 Rackwood Bonnie Lass f.2019

FP5345 Rackwood Maggie May f.2010

Dam: FP3487* Rackwood Maydew, Sire: Wellbrow Samson FP70661C*

Maggie is a thick set pony, very much like her father, but with the additional height from her mother and has matured at 13.2hh. She has many of the qualities of her mother including her sensible outlook and good movement. She was not handled very much as a foal, yearling or two year old so everything was very new to her in the spring of 2013 when she was taken to her first show. She made me extremely proud by winning many awards, for example: in 2013 Great Yorkshire Show: 1st Prize Fell 2&3 yrs; Hexham Native Show: 1st Prize M&M Large Youngstock & M&M Supreme Champion; 2018: South Cumbria FPS Show: 1st Prize Mare 4 yrs +, In-hand Champion, Supreme Show Champion; 2019 FPS Breed Show: 1st Prize Mare 8yrs+.

Maggie May in 2013 at the Breed Show.

All text and photos courtesy of Eileen Walker and her Rackwood Stud web site

FP5345 Rackwood Maggie May at Wolsingham 2013.

Brackenbank Amos FP71039C* f.2007, by Murthwaite Look At Me FP51001C* out of FP3463 Brackenbank Rosie, at the Stallion Show with his breeder David Wilkinson. He was the stallion at the Rackwood stud between 2010 and 2015. Photo, courtesy of Eileen Walker

Lownthwaite

Thomas Wales and Joe Relph

Thomas Wales, on the left, was the son of Harry Wales and brother of Frank, FPS judge and Master of Cumberland Farmers Foxhounds. Joe Relph, Fell pony breeder 1930s-1950s with the Birkett Bank prefix, was secretary of the FPS before Sylvia McCosh. Photo courtesy of Christine Morton

Harry Wales's shepherding pony by Peepings Swell. Frank Wales remarked in his interview for Hoofprints in Eden, "It would be one of the most famous ponies. It would win at London quite a lot. In 1940s Dad got £40 for it."

Frank Wales and his daughter Christine with Johnnie Walker 4140 f.1958, by Master John 2883 out of 9773 Townend Polly V.

Johnnie Walker was sold in 1966 to the millionaire horse-breeder and racing enthusiast EP Taylor of Windfield Farms, Canada. Taylor had already bought a couple of Fells in 1947/48. At the request of FPS Secretary Peggy Crossland, Frank Wales took Johnnie Walker and 2 yearlings to the Ponies of Britain Show run by Glenda Spooner on Ascot Racecourse. EP Taylor bought Johnnie Walker for the record sum of £500, and a yearling for £300. The change of ownership was entered in the Stud Book in March 1967 but Johnnie Walker's foals in Canada were not registered. He left 19 foals in Britain before his export.

11590 Lownthwaite Ann (by Blakebeck Boy 2842 out of 8919 Lownthwaite Swell by Moss Hawk 2430) with Christine Wales, receiving the winner's trophy at Penrith Show from Mrs Hasell of Dalemain. Photo, Christine Morton

Lownthwaite Rob 3960 (by Blakebeck Boy 2842 out of 8694 Lownthwaite Beauty), ridden by Molly Laing's daughter Sally. "He hunts regularly, sometimes carrying Sally's father who is Master of the Liddesdale Fox Hounds, and jumps across country with the best. He completed the 40 mile Golden Horse Shoe ride at Bainbridge in 1966, and competes regularly in cross country events in the Ettrick Forest Team." (1968 FPS Newsletter). Rob's name is on the trophy that the Society now awards each year to the pony that does the most to publicise the breed outside the show ring.

Alison Morton with FP1820 Lownthwaite Duchess (by Townend Samuel FP140C* out of 15145 Lownthwaite Sultana). The photo was taken just before Duchess went to the Queen in August 1994

Peepings Raven FP569C, by Lunesdale Jerry 6841 out of FP1720 Peepings Wild Rose. Peepings Raven sired 84 foals carrying the Lownthwaite prefix. Here he was being shown at the Stallion Show by David Howe, with breeder Jos Dargue (in the deerstalker hat) watching from the ringside. Spectators also included Bill Steadman, Ted Atkinson, Tommy Atkinson, Doug Braithwaite, Bob Coatsworth and daughter Eileen, and Mike Allen. Photo, Ruth Eastwood

FP1985* Lownthwaite Bramble f1990, by Townend Samuel FP140C* out of 17829 Lownthwaite Star Blossom; above, at Penrith Show, ridden by Alison Morton. Photo, courtesy of Christine Morton

Bramble had 8 foals, including FP4050 Lownthwaite Finger Print, here winning the traditional class at the North West Driving Club Show in 2011, driven by Alison Morton; Christine Morton as groom. Photo, Rob Bernard.

Alison Morton with her 5 year old mare FP3831 Lownthwaite Eden bred by her grandfather the late Mr H.F Wales. By Peepings Raven FP569C* out of FP2327* Lownthwaite Lace, L Eden won the Mountain and Moorland In-hand Championship at the Northern Counties Pony Association winter show at Greenlands on 11th November 2007. L Eden also qualified for the 2008 Ponies UK Winter Championships and Pony of the Year Show. Photo, FPS Photo Gallery

Alison Bell (nee Morton) with the 2019 Youngstock Points Award winner FP6226 Lownthwaite Britannia f.2016, by Townend Pirate FP71868C* out of FP3911 Lownthwaite P&O (by Peepings Raven) Photo, FPS Magazine

FP1716* Lownthwaite Orange Blossom, f.1988

Victoria Tollman

Sire: Townend Samuel FP140C, Dam: FP1103 Lownthwaite Apple Blossom

Bred by Mr. H. Frank Wales of the Lownthwaite stud in the UK, Orange Blossom was imported to North America by the late Lyle & Mary Nygaard of Newfarm, in Florida.

Lownthwaite Orange Blossom's dynasty is full of foals, firsts, and accolades. Trained for driving, Blossom was the first Fell pony exhibited and shown in Florida. She still holds the top producer in North America record with 14 foals. However it was her early foals born at Newfarm that have created the majority of her dynasty, a legacy that currently encompasses over 100 North American Fell ponies.

FP1716 Lownthwaite Orange Blossom at a driving clinic at New Farm, Florida, in 1994. For harness enthusiasts - she is put to a 4 wheeled carriage, so the fixed backband is appropriate; I have no doubt that during the clinic the shafts would have been raised several inches at the tugs to bring them and the breeching into a more efficient position. Photo courtesy of Victoria Tollman.*

Foal Highlights

FP2443* Newfarm Valencia f.1993 by Tarnbeck Lightning FP460C*

As Blossom's firstborn Newfarm Valencia was also the first Fell Pony foal born in the USA and registered with FPS. Valencia had 5 progeny and 40 further descendants. Valencia was purchased by Victoria Tollman (BroughHill Fells) and was the first Fell for her breeding program. Progeny of note are BroughHill Hadrian's Wall: 23 progeny with 18 additional descendants = 41 – which includes gr gr gr grand-progeny (5th gen) for Blossom as recently as 2019. Total Valencia descendants to date = 45.

BroughHill Hadrian's Wall FP50964C* f.1999 by Waverhead Robbie FP50109G*. Hadrian is Valencia's firstborn and BroughHill Fell Farm's first foal. Hadrian was exported as a weanling from BroughHill in North Carolina, USA to Ontario, Canada, to Joan O'Brien,

Deerstone ponies. Hadrian produced several Canadian foals before he was exported back to the USA to Rene Bender, FellLegend, of northern California. With Rene, Hadrian embarked upon a winning career under saddle in open pony & M&M licensed shows/classes on the US West Coast, including winning High Point & Performance Fell at age 20 at the Welsh Pony CAC M&M show in 2019. In 1996, Hadrian's portrait made the cover of national publication "Horse Illustrated" magazine. Hadrian also established his own dynasty with 23 foals to date and 18 additional progeny including several 5th generation as recently as 2019.

Blossom Foal #3 1996 Colt Newfarm Midsummers Night FP50613C*

-- a.k.a. "Deryni" (12 progeny + 13 additional descendants)

Deryni progeny totals 12 to date with 13 additional descendants for a total of 25 including some 4th generation

-- first North American bred stallion licensed by FPS

-- first Fell pony anywhere to use Artificial Insemination; producing 5 foals in 2000 by pasture breeding, cooled, & frozen semen & with a 100% conception rate.

-- first Fell pony ever inspected by the North American Sportpony Registry (a division of the American Warmblood Registry) where he went NASR Reserve Champion Pony in 2000

-- first (and only) Fell stallion ever accepted by the Kentucky Horse Park Breeds Barn where he was in the all-season display and exhibition as a ride & drive pony, including sidesaddle.

Deryni being driven at the Kentucky Horse Park by RK Walker, the Park's Equine Operations Manager.

Blossom Foal #4 1998 Filly - FP3161* Newfarm Minneola

(5 progeny + 9 additional descendants)

Minneola was sold to Wendy Ihlang (Mustahevonen) of Washington State, where she had 5 foals which produced an additional 9 descendants including several 4th generations.

Blossom Foal #5 1999 Filly - FP3355* Newfarm Apple Blossom

(1 progeny +14 additional descendants, including some 5th generation as recent as 2021)

Apple Blossom was also sold to Wendy Ihlang. Apple Blossom produced a single son, Mustahevonen Rheged's Pippin FP70241C*, to carry on with 14 additional descendants, mostly under the prefex Royalcrest, for John Rutledge of Arizona.

Foals #6-#14 Newfarm Apple Blossom and her 2nd foal Newfarm Storm were sold in 2000 to Mary Jean Gould-Earley (Laurelhighland) of Pennsylvania, along with several other ponies when Newfarm liquidated and retired. Blossom went on to produce 9 more foals for Laurelhighland:

FP5770* Laurelhighland Duchess, f.2012

Laurelhighland Lucky Charm FP71432C*, f.2009

FP4908* Laurelhighland Clementine , f.2008

Laurelhighland Duke II FP71066G* , f.2007

FP4476* Laurelhighland Lilibet, f.2006

Laurelhighland Beau FP70683G*, f.2005

FP4035* Laurelhighland Rose Petal, f.2004

Laurelhighland Duke FP70043C*, f. 2002

Laurelhighland Knight Waver FP51088C*, f. 2000

Two of those 9 went on to produce 6 descendants, 5 of them out of Laurelhighland Rose Petal after she was sold to breeder Rene Bender (FellLegend) in Oregon.

In North America the influence of Waverhead lines is strong, particularly through Laurelhighland's imports of Waverhead Model IV FP51000G* (now gelded) and Waverhead Robbie FP50109G* (ditto) who are in the pedigree of more than a third of the foals being born there. However, Lownthwaite Orange Blossom was behind 17.5% of the 2019 foals [ref J Morrissey]. She has second-generation progeny under such stud names as Mustahevonen (Wendy Ihlang), Laurelhighland (Mary Jean Gould-Earley), Moonlit (Elise Miller), Willowtrail and Turkeytrot (Jenifer Morrissey), Deerstones (Canada, Joan O'Brien), Kelmscott (Robyn Metcalfe), FellLegend (Rene Bender) and Majestic (Dan Shanahan).

FP3314* Lownthwaite Monarch f.1999

Monarch was also imported from Lownthwaite to North America by Dr Gould-Earley, but she is only distantly related to Orange Blossom. Through her sire Linnel Rapier II, FP50212C*, Monarch traces to Mighty Atom via Flora III *qv*; plus Johnnie Walker, Master John, and a long Sleddale line through Sleddale Ruth.

Her dam Church Farm Jennifer goes back through the grandsire to Greenholme and Heltondale lines and to Glenwelt, and on the granddam's side to Lunesdale, Guards and Lownthwaite.

Monarch has had 10 foals and there are 12 progeny in the next generation, but she has had only 3 fillies, of whom only one has had a foal, and very few of her colts are entire, so her influence is not widespread. However, Laurelhighland Romany Boy FP70430C* sired by Peepings Raven FP569C*, with whom Monarch was in foal in 2004 prior to export, has 11 progeny.

FP3314* Lownthwaite Monarch, by Linnel Rapier II FP50212C* out of FP1350* Church Farm Jennifer. Photo courtesy of Lori Welbig

FP3715 - Brackenbank Megan f.2002, by Tunstall Jake FP50777C* out of FP2507 Brackenbank Primrose, ridden by Philippa Coates. She was Reserve Ridden Supreme Champion at the Northern Counties Pony Association (Cumbria Branch) Annual Show in June 2007.

Photo, FPS web site Photo Gallery.

Lownthwaite Boy / Summerhouse Greta

Frances Wales riding Lownthwaite Boy 3524, f. 1951. Photo about 1958, from Christine Morton.

When Christine Morton sent me this photo of her sister Frances Wales riding Lownthwaite Boy, about 1958, she was unsure whether Lownthwaite Boy was ever registered. However, I looked, and he was. Lownthwaite Boy 3524, f. 1951, was by Blakebeck Boy 2842 out of 8687 Lownthwaite Bess. He sired just one filly, 12006 Downhill Vera, out of 10161 Lownthwaite Lorna.

Downhill Vera, however, had 3 fillies:

13512 Winston Charm

14459 Wharton Surprise

15044 Winston Jewel

These mares in turn bred ponies for Hillhead, Hylands and Greenbell studs. Still, it was an unremarkable line, I thought, and I was probably not going to include the old photo at all.

However, while I was writing this book, Kirsty Budd sent me a photo of Summerhouse Greta FP5652 (left) taking 3rd place at the Horse of The Year Show in the "Search For A Star" Working Pony class in 2021. And when I looked at Greta's pedigree, there was the link:

Summerhouse Greta is by Underwoods Gideon FP50531C* out of FP4269 Rulewater Lucy. She traces through the tail female line all the way back to Lownthwaite Boy:

FP5652 Summerhouse Greta, bred by Peter Boustead, by Underwoods Gideon FP50531C out of FP4269 Rulewater Lucy.*
Photo courtesy of Kirsty Budd

FP5652 Summerhouse Greta /
FP4269 Rulewater Lucy /
FP1530 Edenside Tegra /
16954 Greenbell Jewel /
14459 Wharton Surprise /
12006 Downhill Vera by Lownthwaite Boy 3524.

Brackenbank

David and Katherine Wilkinson have owned, bred and shown Fell Ponies for almost 40 years, now with their daughter, Megan. David is a Fell Pony Society Panel judge and has served on the FPS Council since 1999, and Katherine is the FPS Secretary.

David Wilkinson with FP3006 Brackenbank Romany f.1997, by Waverhead Prince II FP234C* out of FP2158* Brackenbank Mayblossom (by Heltondale Duke IV FP227C*)

Romany has always been a favourite mare at Brackenbank. She is very intelligent, taking anything asked of her in her stride.

She has been very successful in the show ring, winning championships at many shows throughout Cumbria, as well as Fell Pony Champion at Lowther in 2004 and a regular prize winner at the FPS breed show.

She bred 4 foals from 2003 to 2006, Maggie May, Suzanna, Romany's Prince (see next page) and Chloe. Then she was a ridden/hacking /showing pony, including young handlers, fancy dress and junior ridden, from 2007 to 2014.

FP6447 Brackenbank Gracie f.2017, by Wellbrow Lancashire Lad FP71670C* out of Romany

She bred a further 4 foals from 2015 to 2019, Demelza (right), Gracie, Jessica and Tiger Roll, and is now retired and loving life.

FP70597C* Brackenbank Romany's Prince f.2005, by Murthwaite Look at Me FP51001C* out of Romany. Now in USA, with 29 foals, mostly for the Laurelhighland stud in Pennsylvania. Photo, courtesy of Mary Jean Gould-Earley

FP6161 Brackenbank Demelza f.2015, by FP72037G* Brackenbank Oscar (by FP825C* Lownthwaite Gary) out of Romany

Brackenbank Tiger Roll FP73132G, f.2019 by Jamathad Tyson FP72392C* (by Lunesdale Black Ice II FP71130C*) out of Romany

Text and photographs courtesy of Katherine Wilkinson.

Greenholme

15030 Lady of Greenholme f.1971, by Heltondale Ranger 4778 (by Heltondale Mountain Prince 4184) out of 12839 Heltondale Lady III (by Packway Royal 3276) exhibited by Jeff Potter and winning at Greenholme Show, around 1975. Photo, courtesy of Bill & Isobel Potter

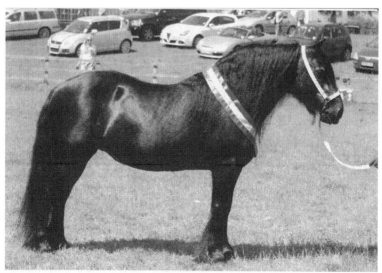

FP2249 Greenholme Kite f.1992, at 21 years old: Reserve Champion VHS Olympia Veteran Qualifier, Towy Valley Riding Club Show. Kite is by Heltondale Ted FP487C* out of FP1854 Greenholme Diane, and owned by Oliver Mockridge. Photo, FPS Magazine, Anthony Reynolds

Greenholme Lilly FP2396 f.1993, by Lunesdale Mountain Mist (by Lunesdale Henry) out of FP1934 Orton Hall Belle (by Htd Black Prince III). Right, as a 3 year old; left, as a mature mare on Birkbeck fell. Photos, courtesy of Bill & Isobel Potter

Greenholme Queen Bea FP5338 f.2010, by Greenholme Look At Me FP70294C*, out of FP4101 - Greenholme Whisper (by Lunesdale Redstart FP50708C*). Owned by K Scorey, shown by Philip Ward-Burton, winner of the Mares 4-8 years old class at the FPS Southern Show in 2017. Photo, FPS Magazine

FP4791 Greenholme Caitlin f.2008, by Greenholme Look At Me FP70294C* out of FP4105
Greenholme Wishful (by Murthwaite Black Bobby FP50558G*). Photo, Ruth Eastwood

Bred by Miss RJ Potter, Caitlin won the filly foal class at the 2008 FPS Breed Show. She was Champion at the FPS Sandringham show in 2016 as well as winning the Horse of the Year show qualifier at the FPS Breed show that year, ridden by Tamsyn Bell-Heather for owner Joanna Minns.

South Cumbria Show Ridden Champion 2008, FP3556 Greenholme Sapphire, by Greenholme
Mikado FP50337C* out of FP2139 Heltondale Mini (by Heltondale Rover IV FP480C).
Rider Mrs L Welch. Photo, FPS Magazine

175

Greenholme Kipper FP6238 f.2016, by Greenholme Diego FP71371C* out of FP4539 Salisbury Pippa (Drybarrows Rusty FP606C x FP70330 Greenholme Vicky) seen here with Anna Metcalfe at the Great Yorkshire Show. Owned by Bev and Anna Metcalfe. Photo, 1st Class Images

Kipper's dam Greenholme Vicky was by Severnvale Grey Bobby FP50712C* out of FP3284 Greenholme Bonny;

> G. Bonny was by Tebay Paddy FP512G* x FP1533 Greenholme Beauty II;

>> G. Beauty II was by Moorhouse Black Prince 6117 x 15783 Greenholme Carol;

>>> G. Carol was by Heltondale Rambler II 4749 x one of Bill Potter's foundation mares, 12840 Heltondale Lilly (p174)

A MARE MISCELLANY

8086 Linnel Sandpiper f.1945, by Linnel Romany II 2400 out of 6789 Dalemain Sapphire, at the 1948 NPS Show at Roehampton. Sandpiper was exported to Australia. Photo, W Rouch & Co, from the Charlton Collection

Dalemain Love-in-the-Mist 9845, f.1951, champion 2 year old filly by Dalemain Groundsel 2703 out of 6798 Dalemain Sapphire by Linnel Lingcropper 1621.

8575 Linnel Flighty f.1947, by Linnel Gipsy Lad 2630 out of 7421 Linnel Kathleen (by Linnel Gallant Boy 1704). Photo, Charlton Collection

15515 Robbswater Rachel and her 1991 foal Robbswater Rowan FP848G, by Heltondale Josh FP587C*. Photo, Ruth Eastwood

High Heath Ponies
Julia Woods (Spacey)

The top pony is FP1160 Capenoch Carlotta (Heltondale Rambler II 4749 x 17517 Leithenwater Caradale).

The pony in the middle is 17620 High Heath Edwina (Bassenbeck Jasper 6250 x 15747 High Heath Heidi), owned and bred by Janice Howard.

The 3 below are full sisters 17620 High Heath Edwina and 18140 High Heath Edwina II, and the stallion 7059 High Heath Gunner (Bassenbeck Jasper 6250 x 16544 Lunesdale Bunty). Gunner was the sweetest, kindest pony I ever had.

I showed all of them in the late 80's and early 90's. I was Julia Spacey then! They all won Ridden, Working Hunter Pony and Dressage classes.

The two mares were known as Elkie (Brooks) and Whitney (Houston) because of their manes!

Whitney had her photo in Horse and hound having been Champion ridden Mountain and Moorland pony at Ponies of Britain, at Ascot.

Foggy Gill Dapper 18118 f.1980

Foggy Gill Dapper, by Sleddale King of the Fell 5902 out of 17759 Peggy of Foggy Gill. Dapper was bred in 1980 by Mr H Tunstall, Fell End, Kirkby Stephen. She is seen here with her first foal in 1986, for Janet Wood (Ralfland), the bay Ralfland Tansy FP1792, by Heltondale Hero 6908.
In the ownership of Janet's sister Marion Robinson (Orton Hall), Dapper had 10 more foals, of which 5 were grey, 4 black and 1 brown. Photo, Joanne Exley

Ralfland Tansy FP1762, Dapper's first foal and the only bay. She is seen here with her 7th foal Ralfland Bracken FP2868 by Drybarrows Rusty FP606C , foaled 1996. Tansy has had 12 foals in all, 7 black and the rest bay. Photo, Janet Wood

Dapper's second foal, FP1936* Orton Hall Dolly f.1988, by Heltondale Rover IV FP480C. Bred by Marion Robinson. Dolly had 9 foals, 8 of them with the Llancloudy stud for Mrs Gina Feakins.

Dapper's 4th foal, Orton Hall Danny FP778C* f.1990, by Heltondale Black Prince III FP188C* seen here doing a demonstration with his owner, Pat Burge. Danny was a tall Fell, at least 14.1hh, possibly inheriting his height from his sire. He sired 10 foals in North America.

18092 Swindale Rose, by Sleddale King of the Fell 5902 out of 14629 Sleddale Dainty VIII. Barbara Bell is holding Rose for her owner and driver, Hazel Hindmarch. I believe her mane had been plaited, here; when I owned her, her hair was completely straight. Photo, Ruth Eastwood

I owned Rosie from 1983 to 1989. According to her papers the sire and dam were full siblings, both by Heltondale Sonny Boy 4473 out of 13164 Sleddale Dainty VIII. Rosie had two foals for Hazel Hindmarch, but neither had any progeny. There were two other ponies from the pairing of Sleddale King of the Fell and Sleddale Dainty VIII: Swindale Stroller 6901G, and 17222 Swindale Brown Girl whose line went to the Murthwaite stud via Foggy Gill Brenda.

14357 Townend Princess f.1970, by Lunesdale Richard 4637 out of 12828 Waverhead Princess. Champion mare, owned and exhibited by Don Crow.

Mr. Crow, having won the Dales Championship, achieves a "double" by taking the Fell Championship with his 4-year-old "Townend Princess", out of "Waverhead Princess". These mares and the Dales Champion all emanate from three top North Country studs — Wheatside, Townend and Waverhead.

FP1756 Drybarrows Duchess II by a 3 year old Heltondale colt out of FP1298 Drybarrows Purple Heather. At home with breeder Chris Thompson in May 1992. Photo, FPS web site

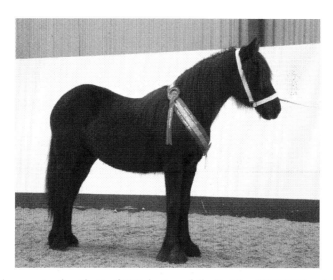

FP6177 Drybarrows Another Chapter f.2015, by Carrock I'm Yer Man FP51327C* out of FP5407 Drybarrows Collean, champion at the 2017 Youngstock Show. Photo, FPS Magazine, Claire Simpson

12886 Greenfield Ruby f.1964 by Linnel Fox 4296 out of 10918 Roundthwaite Ruby) at FPS Breed Show at Brougham Hall Farm in 1975. She took part in the Lowther tableau in 1975 as a pack pony; represented Fells at the NPS Stand at the Royal Show; was 2nd in her class at the Breed Show and won the Novice and Children's riding classes there.

Photo Charles Donaldson; John Slater/Margaret Bainbridge.

12967 Greenfield Mayflower, f.1965, by Linnel Fox 4296 out of 12045 May Queen. Foal, Greenfield Dandelion 6769, f.May 1977, by Townend Prince III 5680. 13172 Greenfield Beauty is in the background. Photo John Slater/Margaret Bainbridge.

15621 Greenfield Polly (A), f.1973, by Htd Sonny Boy 4473 out of 12922 Snip of Wharton (IS). Photo courtesy of John Slater/Margaret Bainbridge.

FP2888 Lunesdale Honey f.1996, by Lunesdale Henry 6932 out of FP1896 Lunesdale Rosebud (by Heltondale Hero 6908 out of FP1871 Lunesdale White Rose). Competing in the FPS classes at Lowther Show, 2004, ridden by Bev Metcalfe. Photo, Sue Millard

Breed show Champion 2014, FP4250 Banksgate Galway Girl f.2006, by Townend Rally FP51093G* out of FP3792 Banksgate Bonny Lass (by Murthwaite Jack Snipe FP50979C*). Bred by Catherine Ashcroft; shown by Tony Ashcroft. Photo, FPS Magazine

2017 breed show Ridden Champion and reserve Supreme, FP5287 Raisbeck Calico f.2010 by Murthwaite Look at Me FP51001C* out of FP3481 Raisbeck Casino (by Rylstone Black Knight FP50148C*). Bred by Diana Slack; rider, Miss A Dickinson. Photo, Claire Simpson

THE LAST 30 YEARS

FIS - Slowly Winning the Battle
Sue Millard

Fell ponies are tough. They seldom ail much. However, there is one problem which came to light in 1993 and since 1995 has occasionally made the national press. This is a condition now known as Foal Immunodeficiency Syndrome (FIS): "a congenital fatal immunodeficiency that commonly leads to anaemia and lymphopenia" (Thomas et al., 17 May 2003).

It is an auto-immune defect, and foals die from random opportunistic infections. "This immunodeficiency is unlike any other seen in the horse or indeed any other species, including man." (Carter, cited in FPS *Jubilee Celebration Book*, 2002)

It was first drawn to the attention of the veterinary profession by Paul May:

> The first time I was aware of it was in 1993. As long ago as that. Probably three years before that, we'd been seeing individual foals, and trying to make a judgement as to what was going on. The thing with the Syndrome is that, if you've seen them as an individual, there's nothing; there's frustration there because you haven't cured it, but there's nothing that rings any great alarm bells—if they die quickly. But if they drag on and on and on and you see the anaemia and you see how pale they become then you realise that this is something new. It took two cases—it was the third case when I realised that what we were seeing was something that didn't fit into any of the normal foal diseases.
>
> If you look at what happens to them, they get recurrent diseases, recurrent infections; well, you can get that in certain individuals anyway, maybe ones that didn't get the full dose of colostrum, they are always weak. But by the time you've come to the third one, bearing in mind that we've said they are robust and hardy anyway, that really did ring alarm bells. You can allow the odd one, say, "Okay that was a weak foal, and couldn't throw off infections," but by the time you've got to the third one something starts to worry you. And then if you make it survive long enough that you start to see the anaemia as well, then that's when alarm bells ring. Then history takes over …
>
> In the early days it was all very gloomy. Because we didn't know what was causing it, we didn't know how to go forward with it. That's the trouble when you've got a completely novel disease, you can't predict anything. (Paul May, MRCVS; in 2005)

Breeders leave their mares to foal outdoors, and often on the fell. They bring them home just for service and turn them out again once they are served. Because of that, and the fact that ponies are normally run as part of a farm which also suffers losses around lambing and calving, occasional foal deaths are accepted, resignedly, as a natural occurrence. Unexplained losses in the first few months of life could just as easily fit with an accident as into the Syndrome pattern, so identifying a single common cause was difficult, and the Syndrome might therefore not have come to public notice but for the work of Paul May.

Certainly in the early stages, they all seemed to scour. They all seemed to scour about the time of the foal heat. Most foals scour at that age anyway. Speaking to breeders before that time – they'd come in and say, "Oh, I've got a foal's scoured, I need some scour medicine" or whatever; and you'd do that and you'd never hear any more. Some of those won't have survived. Some of them will have done. Natural losses are accepted – "Well, we didn't win with this one. I've got another twenty – let's move on to them." And it isn't until you bunch everybody's results together and realise there is something going on – unless lots of neighbours got together and said, "What have you lost this year?" – unless that happened, you'd know very little. (Paul May, MRCVS; in 2005)

Horses are not prolific animals. Mares may miss a year of production for several reasons. Examination of published Fell Pony Society foaling records in the early 20th century indicates that still births, "slipped foals", and neo-natal deaths were fairly common. Live foaling percentages for a travelling stallion could be as low as 29%, while in 1916 the FPS records show that 313 mares were served of whom 175 had live foals, making the average foaling percentage for mares 55.9%. In 1918, only 43% of served mares had living offspring.

Neonatal losses are a known risk in farming. Taking figures such as these into account, it is hardly surprising that modern losses, some of which may have been from the Syndrome, were not always recognised as such by breeders. The symptoms of the Syndrome could vary and foals died from many different infections.

They present differently every year. What you tend to get is, you get one year when they all do one thing. One year they're all scoured, or they'll all cough; but they all do different things in different years. Two years ago we had a whole lot with arthritis, swollen joints. You can get them as early as five days. The whole thing about it is there are no rules in it. Okay, there are the average cases; you can say, yes, the average doesn't present till a month, and dies four weeks later, or whatever, but the youngest we've had was five days of age and died overnight. We've had one that didn't show until it was twelve weeks of age. Normally you can say by the time you've got through eight weeks you're safe, yet suddenly at twelve weeks it started up. So there is an enormous range there. (Paul May, MRCVS; in 2005)

Breeders and vets formulated a range of hypotheses as to the Syndrome's origin and how long it had been in existence, but the principal working assumption was that it was genetic. There are potential sources in genetic "bottlenecks" (such as might be caused by low numbers in the breeding population, or extremely widespread use of just a few stallions) one of which occurred in the years around the Second World War, and another in the 1950s when, under the Enclosure scheme, single stallions were able to be extremely influential. In both systems, some were used for three or more successive years. However, genetic problems could equally have arisen much earlier than that: there were FPS comments as early as 1914 about the stock being potentially inbred, due to the sire lines then nearly all coming from Blooming Heather 325. In 1916 some stallions were so heavily used that the Board of Agriculture was moved to propose that no Fell should stand as a Premium stallion in a district for more than 4 years in succession. So it is difficult—and pointless—to try to identify which animal might have been the historic source of the faulty gene, or genes.

> What the researchers were trying to do was just to work back by mathematical prediction; they reckon it's some time, some people even say between the two wars, in the late 30s or early 40s. The whole breed at that stage was very poorly represented—what we are assuming is that this is a genetic mutation—it would allow that genetic mutation to become easily distributed through the breed. A lot of people said, "Well, why has it suddenly appeared?" But you don't see a recessive genetic problem in any sort of numbers until it is pretty much right through the breed. (Paul May, MRCVS; in 2005)

A Recessive Gene

Various teams worked on the Syndrome problem over the next decade and a half. Serious funding for research was needed. "Fell Pony 2000" raised money for the work and the Rare Breeds Survival Trust offered its expertise, proposing breeding strategies for use once there was a test for the disease. In 2004 an American multidisciplinary research team became involved, hoping that their findings might be used to inform research into certain forms of congenital bone marrow failure in children. However, the major work over the years was conducted in the UK at Liverpool University's Leahurst Unit on the Wirral and at the Animal Health Trust (AHT) at Newmarket, with funding from The Horse Trust.

The Liverpool team was led initially by Professor Derek Knottenbelt and Professor Gareth Thomas at the University's Leahurst veterinary campus. The team was later headed by the AHT's Dr June Swinburne, in collaboration with Professor Stuart Carter of the University of Liverpool, and Dr Laura Fox-Clipsham.

> For a while we thought the numbers (of syndrome foals) were reducing; but I think a lot of it just depends on how many are being reported. And it got so much bad press that you can't really blame people for not reporting them, because it was attracting all this ridiculous coverage: "Fell Pony Plague!" At one point somebody was publishing information saying there was a secondary syndrome that they might get in adulthood. It was a total fabrication – wherever they got that from I don't know, but scaremongering like that can destroy a breed. A lot of people were saying that the breed would die out because of the scaremongering, not because of the disease.

> There is all the pressure of trying to get a test out so that if anyone's worried they can get a test on the foal at an early stage. Once you've got a test, that's fine – but what are you going to test? Are you going to test the parents? Are you going to test the stallions? Are you going to test the foals when they're born? The foals when they're born, that's not controversial at all, that's fine; that just allows people to know whether they're clear, or no, they've got a carrier. Testing stallions is politically very difficult, because what are you going to do with the results? You could say, well, nobody needs to know if it's a negative; but if everybody goes around publicising

that their stallion is clear, then for anyone who remains silent the assumption will be made that theirs is a carrier.

You look back over ten or fifteen years of it and ask, "What has it actually done to the breed? Has it severely weakened it?" I don't think it has had a major effect on it. It's caused a lot of attention to be brought to focus on the breed; but there's still plenty of Fell ponies going to shows. They're definitely not dying out. (Paul May, MRCVS)

While the research was still being done, some owners castrated stallions that had produced Syndrome foals. Breeders also expressed a fear that the Society would impose a blanket policy of not breeding from carrier ponies, and that good qualities in carrier animals would be lost forever to the breed. Would Fell pony breeders have to stop using their best ponies because of a theoretical 1 in 4 chance of a sick foal? They were all undoubtedly worrying about that when they made their breeding decisions.

Saffron Townsend of the Rare Breeds Survival Trust was cited in the *FPS Jubilee Celebration Book*, 2002, as saying that in small breeding populations such as the Fell, genetic diversity can be lost much more quickly than in large ones, and genetic "erosion" can lead to a poorer quality of animals and a higher incidence of genetic disease. Because of this, if Syndrome carrier animals were simply dropped from the breeding programme, this would drastically reduce the genetic diversity—it would cause another genetic "bottleneck" that might prove to be a very much worse choice than continuing to breed from carriers.

It came as no surprise that some popular stallions and prizewinning mares showed themselves to be carriers by producing foals that died with all the characteristics of the Syndrome. Paul May discussed this in his interview in 2005:

What it's going to need is some very very clear thinking and bold and brave enterprise, people going out there who will say, "Look, you will destroy the breed if you just say, 'We are only breeding from A1 clear stallions!'" because those stallions may not be good breed type anyway. You look, for example, at the scrapie testing in sheep, and they are saying that a lot of the good sheep are the ones that are poorer in genetic resistance to scrapie.

There is no reason why good breed characteristics should be linked with the syndrome, no reason whatsoever, but it does seem to be linked to a strong breed type of some kind. (Paul May MRCVS)

Dr Gareth Thomas originally estimated that 33-50% of Fell ponies were carriers for the condition (FPS *Jubilee Celebration Book*, 2002). DNA testing eventually showed this to be close to the truth. The research area was also widened with the discovery of the Syndrome in Dales ponies and a small percentage of it in coloured cobs that had Fell ponies in their background. Through the work done by Liverpool and the AHT, FIS is now known to be caused by a single mutation in the sodium/myo-inositol cotransporter gene (SLC5A3). This gene plays a vital role in the regulatory response in many tissues including lymphoid tissues.

FIS is confirmed as an autosomal recessive trait, meaning a foal can only be affected if the foal inherits the disease from both parents. Animals that are carriers do not have any symptoms associated with FIS and will live normal healthy lives. The genetic mutation can manifest itself whenever two animals carrying the mutated gene or genes are mated. This is a 'roll of the dice' with every mating; whether previous foals from that mare or stallion have been clear, carrier or Syndrome does not matter. A mating has the same chances every time.

1. The foal from a carrier-to-carrier mating has a 1 in 4 chance of not inheriting the faulty gene. It will never produce a foal that will die of the disease, though it might produce a carrier if mated to a carrier.

2. The foal has a 1 in 2 chance of inheriting the gene from one parent, and thus being a carrier as they are; but barring "normal" risks and accidents, it will not die in foalhood.

3. It also has a 1 in 4 chance of inheriting the gene twice, once from each parent, and then it will display symptoms of the Syndrome and die.

Even from a carrier-to-carrier mating there are 3 chances in 4 that the foal will grow normally and survive. It was estimated during the research period that fewer than 1 in 10 of Fell pony foals born each year actually died because of FIS.

The researchers also took pains to point out that *even if* every single Fell pony carried this damaged gene (which is not the case), the breed would not die out. In an absolutely worst-case scenario, *if* every single breeding animal were a carrier (one copy of the defective gene related to FIS), and *if* all matings had therefore to be carrier-to-carrier, even then, the next generation would contain: some "positive" foals who would die of the Syndrome, many ponies that were carriers and also some ponies that were clear, with no copies of the gene. Individual years would vary, but the average over the years would still be 75% survivors - 50% carriers and 25% of the foals being clear. But *not every pony is a carrier*. Even in 2010 the estimate was 39% carriers, ie, 61% were probably clear. Bob Charlton wrote a helpful guide explaining these breeding possibilities, which was posted onto the FPS web site for reference and is still available there as a link on the Health page.

At one time the Fell was in the "endangered" category of the Rare Breeds Survival Trust, which set that category's criteria as 300-500 registered mares of breeding age; a change in the RBST criteria now places the breed in the middle of their three current categories for rare breeds. To put foal numbers into a historical perspective, the 1916 stallion progeny records showed 175 foals born (not all of whom would go on to be registered); whereas the 2002 stud book registered a global foal crop of 274 colts, geldings and fillies. Although actual foaling numbers went down a little in the years preceding 2013, that was due to breeders' response to the global recession, rather than to FIS. The 2021 stud book registered well over 300 foals, a much larger number than was recorded ninety years ago, and Fell ponies nowadays probably do better than they did then in terms of percentage foaling rates.

Successful Research

In January 2010 all the members of the Fell Pony Society Council and the Dales Pony Society Council were invited to attend a meeting with the research team at Leahurst. I was especially happy to revisit this campus, where in 1967 I had done school work experience at the pig research unit and the horse surgical yards. Of course we were all cautiously excited, because surely Professor Carter would only bring together so many people from both breeds if he had significant progress to report?

We were welcomed by Professor Carter and Laura Fox-Clipsham, who had pursued the Syndrome research for her doctorate. They outlined the history of the research and explained that the name had been changed to Foal Immunodeficiency Syndrome (FIS) because the problem was not exclusive to Fells. Finally, they made the announcement that 15 years of research had paid off. By intensively computed analysis of the DNA material, they had pinpointed the gene and the allele within it that carried the lethal flaw. They had been able to construct a test to discover the FIS status of live animals, and it had proved reliable. This test would prevent unnecessary suffering by informing breeders of ponies' FIS status, and enable them to prevent the birth of foals affected with the condition.

A couple of weeks later Fell Pony Society Chairman Miss Longsdon welcomed Professor Carter and Laura Fox-Clipsham, and Dr June Swinburn (Animal Health Trust) to an FPS meeting in Orton Market Hall, where Dr Carter outlined the research into the disease over the past decade and a half. FIS is an autosomal recessive genetic disease probably stemming from one individual with a mutated section of gene 26. This kind of disease, not linked to the sex of the foal and not expressed in any outward form, can spread undetected through many generations of a population without causing a problem. It is likely to have spread during two genetic "bottlenecks" in the 1950s and 1960s when, through the Enclosure system, the breed used relatively few stallions each year.

Laura Fox-Clipsham explained that a foal receives half its genetic makeup from its mother and half from its father. A healthy foal will be born if it receives at least one copy of the dominant gene that produces immunity. Its second copy of the gene can be either another dominant (healthy) gene or a recessive (faulty) gene. The risk of foal death only occurs when two carriers of the mutated gene are bred together – ponies that both carry the recessive as well as dominant genes.

There is a 25% chance in that case of producing a foal that does not receive any copy of the mutated gene (homozygous clear); and a 50% chance of receiving one copy of the mutated gene (heterozygous carrier). Finally it has a 25% chance of receiving two copies of the gene (homozygous carrier), and such a foal will die. The condition is a major consideration for all Fell breeders.

Even a carrier to carrier mating has a 75% chance of producing a healthy foal, but the best choices are a carrier to clear mating or a clear to clear, which will both have a 100% chance of survival. Most importantly, by defining the status of the clear ponies, about which we could previously only make a good guess, we can now make informed choices about breeding. We should be able to avoid ever breeding another Syndrome foal.

The DNA test now identifies genetic status with reference to the Syndrome. It distinguishes the three categories of genetic status: homozygous clear, heterozygous carrier, and homozygous carrier or "Syndrome foal". A reassuring point was that the researchers estimate that at least 60% of ponies in the breed are likely to be free of the defective gene; this was estimated by testing samples from Fells which were not involved in the Syndrome research.

Dr Swinburne said that the test is done, as for a DNA sample, using hair from either the mane or tail, which must be pulled, not cut, because the root of the hair is needed to obtain the DNA. DNA samples already archived with the AHT, for instance from stallion licensing applications, can also be used to determine status. Any age of pony can be tested.

The team said that the ultimate aim for the future would be the elimination of the FIS gene from the Fell pony breeding population. This would require the GRADUAL withdrawal of all carrier ponies from breeding. Dr Carter's hope was to breed no more affected foals.

The large-scale breeders were more cautious. They would not entirely reject carrier-to-carrier matings because these may still give not only live foals but also clear, non-FIS foals —and such foals will carry on good quality lines as well as being FIS-free.

Dr Swinburne agreed with breeders that realistically, preventing the breeding of carriers may in fact be undesirable, particularly if high quality animals may prove to be carriers. The defect is only one aspect of a carrier's genetic make-up and the desirable characteristics carried may outweigh this fault. One advantage which the new carrier test provides is that carriers CAN now be confidently used in breeding programmes by breeding only to clear ponies, with no risk of producing an affected foal.

Extreme reactions by breeders, such as gelding carrier stallions or excluding mares from breeding, would create a rapid reduction in eligible breeding stock, and would in fact replicate the genetic bottleneck that is theorised to have originally spread the FIS gene—thus possibly risking another recessive problem in future generations.

In the long term, the aim for the breed should be to reduce the frequency of carrier-to-carrier and carrier-to-normal matings, to bring FIS down to near zero levels whilst maintaining desirable genes.

The research was made possible thanks to funding from The Horse Trust and the support of the Fell Pony Society, Fell Pony 2000, and the Dales Pony Society who have supplied DNA samples. (from the *Fell Pony Magazine*, Spring 2010)

For breeders the most important point is that the FIS test identifies which of their ponies are clear non-carriers and which carry the Syndrome. There is also a very important welfare aspect: previously, if two carriers were bred together and the resulting foal became ill, you couldn't be sure whether it was a symptom of the Syndrome or just a run of the mill foalhood problem. However, the test can now reveal the foal's FIS status. If it does test positive for FIS the kindest course is to put it down before inevitable further infections cause it more suffering; whereas if it is clear or a carrier, the Syndrome is not the cause of the illness and so treatment is more worthwhile.

Strong Opinions

FIS is a subject that still provokes the expression of strong opinions.

One of the points made over and over during the discussions - before FIS was pinpointed and the carrier test found - was that breeders did NOT want to be told what they should or should not do. The Fell Pony Society has not imposed any restriction on the choice of breeding stock. An FIS test result is confidential and there is no compulsion to make it public - unlike other breed societies (eg of Arabs) who stipulate that recessive genetic flaws must be disclosed to all parties when a breeding is arranged. However, if there's a breeding-age pony for sale and it's tested FIS clear it's obvious that this is going to be mentioned as a selling point.

Breeders with only one or two mares clearly can't afford the larger breeder's approach of "well we lost this one, but we still have twenty" as described by Paul May. They can, however, avoid the risk of losing a foal if they test their mares; if they are clear, then any stallion can be chosen; if they turn out to be carriers, use a stallion advertised as FIS clear.

Those who make their stallions available to outside mares do inform mare owners if the horse the owners ask to use is a carrier, just as they advise on other considerations such as conformation or height. There would be little point in trying to conceal a carrier stallion's status, because once he sired a Syndrome foal the news would go round the small Fell world very quickly. Quite apart from that, stallion owners don't want to risk upsetting a one-mare owner, nor the mare, who would both be distressed by the loss of a foal.

> "There isn't any survived [the Syndrome] yet. My last one was to put down; I kept it alive, it wasn't getting any better and it wasn't getting any worse, so we just put it down. Cause we knew it wasn't going to get any better; it was just hanging on so you might as well put it down at word Go." (Only one breeder discussed the Syndrome during the original interviews, and I chose to leave the identity anonymous here.)

Breeders have received support from the Society, from veterinarians and researchers and from the RBST. Financial support was given to enable high levels of testing during the first 3 years when the test was available. However, what each breeder chooses to do about the Syndrome has more effect than the Syndrome itself on the long-term health of the breed. Any policy imposed on the choice of stallions would narrow the genetic options. The hill breeders do want to be able to breed carrier to carrier *occasionally* where blood lines and quality suggest they should take the risk, hoping for the 1:4 chance that the resulting foal will be FIS clear, and can safely carry forward the good qualities into future generations. It must be stressed that there is no guarantee: every mating involving a carrier is a fresh "roll of the dice", whether the mare or stallion have produced FIS foals or not.

Reporting the effects of the test

Professor Stuart Carter's team published a paper (Veterinary Record, 2013) showing that the number of FIS foals born each year had already dropped since FIS testing started in 2010.

> 1. A large number of ponies have been tested

> 2. The number of FIS foals has dropped dramatically in all breeds tested (only 1 foal tested positive in 2012). This is an excellent outcome and very clear evidence of breeders and scientists working together to improve animal welfare and much credit should go to the owners/ breeders for enabling the research programme and for then conscientiously using the carrier test to stop FIS foals being born.

> Testing of potential breeding ponies will need to be continued as the current breeding strategy (allowing carriers to breed with clears) will not reduce the large numbers of carriers; however, the majority of current breeding ponies have already been tested and it will just be necessary to test new animals selected for breeding in the future.

It has been a long journey to get to this point, but is justification for the considerable efforts of many individuals over many years and the eventual outcome.

Predictably, our breeding recommendations to use carrier-clear matings have not had a rapid impact on the large numbers of FIS carriers … Reducing carrier numbers will take either much longer using the current breeding approach, or a change in breeding strategy to avoid breeding from carriers at all. With the carrier rate so high in the Fell ponies, such a restrictive recommendation would probably be unacceptable to many breeders, and would risk depleting the gene pool. On the other hand, the breeders who choose carrier-clear matings will need to test their offspring to see if their foal is a carrier.

The results are consistent with uptake of the FIS carrier test by the owners of at-risk ponies, and suggest that they have also taken our advice about breeding strategies to reduce the numbers of FIS-positive foals. (*Veterinary Record,* April 13, 2013)

The Society's Advice

If your pony is from two "tested clear" parents your pony will also be clear. TEST if the pony you intend to breed has a carrier parent or a parent of unknown FIS status.

If you put your "tested clear" mare to a "tested clear" stallion:

1. The foal will be clear.

2. It can never produce a foal carrying the FIS gene.

3. There is NO possibility of "throwbacks" to produce an FIS Syndrome foal or a carrier.

You MUST check the mare's and the stallion's status though.

It's impossible to produce an FIS Syndrome foal, or an FIS carrier, IF the test has shown both parents are clear.

There IS always a possibility that paperwork is not correct! - whether by accident or by design.

Don't let anyone tell you that because a mare or a stallion has never produced an FIS foal, it is FIS clear. The "luck of the draw" may have concealed its FIS carrier status. TEST if you are not certain.

ASK TO SEE THE TEST CERTIFICATE and make sure it truly belongs to the animal in question before you decide to breed.

If you have a sick foal and you're not certain of mare's or stallion's FIS status, remember, the test is there to find out whether you have an FIS foal or whether it is suffering from some other illness that needs to be treated. This is an important matter of animal welfare. (FPS web site, Health page)

A Work in Progress

Fifteen years of research and twelve years of test usage have enabled the majority of breeders to avoid producing foals that will die of FIS. They have also gone some way towards excluding the damaged gene from the breed's genetics. Provided the people who breed make sure to test their ponies first to find out their FIS status, and match mare to stallion with regard to the advice given over the past twelve years, they should not ever lose a foal to the Syndrome. The aim is still to breed it out, but it must continue to be done gradually, without severe restrictions that would risk creating another genetic bottleneck in the breed.

Reprinted and updated from *Hoofprints in Eden*, 2nd Ed, 2013

Epigenetics and the Hill-Going Fell Pony
Sue Millard

Part of the "type" of the Fell pony is its mountain-pony hardiness, compactness and heavy winter coat, not to mention the ability to store fat and live off fresh air if need be. It is the harsh environment of living on the hill that "switches on" the Fell pony's genes for survival and keeps them switched on in subsequent generations.

Hill-bred ponies can leave the fell and breed in lowland conditions, and their genes continue to be expressed in "survival mode" in the progeny for a couple of generations. However, the fact of those ponies now living and breeding in a kinder environment will *also* induce a change, the other way, in how their genes behave in their offspring. As more generations are foaled off the fell, the resulting ponies become less typical of the Fell in its native habitat, even though they are still pure-bred. This is the case with colts as well as fillies. It has often been observed that "field ponies" are subtly different from "fell ponies" - taller, for instance, and with less heavy coats - though they still seem to retain the ability to be air ferns!

To quote a 2014 article in Scientific American (about humans):

> "... environmental factors, such as diet in utero, can fundamentally alter the on-off switches that control the activity of male offspring's sperm DNA ... your environment when you are in the womb can not only affect your health but also can permanently alter the information that you pass on to your children when they are conceived, and this affects their health as adults." (Maron, 2014)

This mechanism is the science behind the lowland breeders' long-understood need to go back after a couple of generations to buy breeding stock that has been born in a fell-going herd - and why those herds, and mares and stallions living in high, harsh conditions, are so central to retaining the type of the breed.

The Mountain Answers Monbiot
Sue Millard

I hesitated over including these three pages. I wrote this poem some years ago, prompted first by George Monbiot's fulminations about sheep farmers which seemed an insult to everyone's sorrow at the death of a local Fell pony hill breeder. As I wrote, it also became a eulogy for the Fell pony and for a way of life in the northern hills. I think it needs to be here.

Imagine it, if you can, spoken in the voice of the Howgill Fells.

> *Quote: ...a wildlife desert. Blame Wordsworth.*
> Come to this farm that neighbours the fell wall,
> this tired house roofed with unmatched slates,
> whose barns once served a medieval church
> five days over the mountains to the east.
> Once, two lords with a map could make us all
> Scottish or English at a single stroke –
> cattle and sheep, fell farmers and the fells.
>
> I knew those ancestors. They built this
> in the time of the Restoration;
> the date-stone tells of prosperity
> and the raising of barns; and a thousand years
> of sheepwalks, spinning, cowbells and butter.
>
> Meet the inheritor of my land, their line,
> milking his cows and turning out his tups
> raddle-chested to the autumn flock. He learned
> a story from every grass-blade on my flanks –
> a mere ten thousand years of knowledge – how
> ice, compacted a mile deep, ground smooth
> Silurian grit and sandstone; how snow-melt
> carved my long valleys where his ponies shelter
> from the winds; where screes tumble first in frost;
> which of my slopes will bloom in a dry year;
> which valley bottoms slow the winter floods.

A CENTURY OF FELLS

Quote: hill farming with hefted flocks, and a thriving ecosystem,
are at odds.

He walks my rocks – no peat-core biopsy
needed to tell him where the upland
flora come out first to shout of spring;
why forest never hid my windswept tops;
how the tangle-maned Fell mare and her foal
keep their own ground, and every hill-hardy
tuft of sweet turf ties hoof to heaf, up here
where we are roofed by unhaltered cloud.
I speak to him of childhood, when he chased
fox cubs and black-capped gulls. He remembers
how along that trod, his horse ran away
while sledging home the rusted brackens,
and his father cuffed his head and his grandfather
sent him to the forge with chains to mend.
His adolescent legs took him downhill
in seven-league strides, boots slipping on wild thyme.
If you would listen, every slope of me
would share its ghost.

He was lish then, a prize for any woman,
and a twenty-hour day no trouble;
he walked my tops to gather sheep at dawn,
clipped them and turned them back before the night.
When he ran-out Fell stallions, for the old men
to mate to their tail-swishing squealing mares,
their lust pranced over the green spring grass
and his thighs sprinting beside them
drew the young women, flirting, hungering.

If it weren't for that black dog of his
who growled at wedding photographs,
he could have mounted all their bouldered slopes,
laid them in any of the mossy ghylls,
my autumn turf as velvet as their skin.
But I am his Amazon, his Serengeti.
My rowan trees slim as girls' wrists
hang their red-lipped berries over his head.

SUE MILLARD

Quote: Why should Wordsworth and Ruskin
govern our tastes beyond the grave?
Your paper judgement signed by city hands
can't quantify such men as him. His heart
clings to my base rock like the fossils cling
to the mudstone sea-floor, like the peat
layers years bone-deep with carbon from old stars.

At night, before he struggles into bed,
it's me he studies, and the sky I lean on,
for the presence or the absence of the stars,
feeling the scarf of wind worn on my shoulder
to know what morning weather I will give him.
He crawls my flanks now like a scarlet beetle,
sitting the quad bike sideways. Tamed by pain
he hunts only photographs, and the sun.

He knows Death has him in its cross-hairs
and the hammer is about to fall, but
in spirit he's still climbing to my heights
to fetch his sheep or ponies home for birth,
or crossing the sloped meadows at my feet
cutting the sun-warmed grass for winter hay;
watching colts galloping across the snow
bucking and kicking in a dazzle of light.
He is still naming foals as yet unborn.

Do not presume to tell him how to live.

The Howgill Fells are "remote, exposed, open, unenclosed common land, covered with a seasonally colourful mosaic of upland habitats" - Natural England publication

The quotations are from an article by George Monbiot in *The Guardian* (2013) and on his web site, *https://www.monbiot.com/2013/09/02/obstinate-questionings/*.

The Mountain Answers Monbiot was published in *Writing the Weather* (2017) by the Wordsworth Trust, with photographs of Fell ponies. It is in my collection *Galloway Gate* (2019).

A Cautionary Tale

Sue Millard

Although I have devoted many pages in this book to tracing bloodlines and influences, the further back you go the more likely it is that pedigree data are inaccurate.

The reasons for this are many. There are alternative spellings such as Shepster Boy 910 and "Chepstow Boy", which were probably the same stallion (Shepster="Starling"). There have been simple transcription errors such as Ousel / Gusel, Tallentire / Tallentue, Tebay Campbellton Victor / Tebay Campbell Ton Victor; farm names omitted, owner names omitted. Some errors may have been advertising hype, such as the extended pedigree of The Mikado 200 in the "black stud book", which shows his descent from Old Grey Shales in the grand-dam's sire line - it does stretch belief that 5 generations of ponies would span 134 years.

We will often come to a full stop when we work back to the years of the Inspection Scheme, by which typey but unregistered mares could be adopted into the breed and their progeny "bred up" to full pedigree. Often there is no background data for these mares, and two influential 20thC stallions had IS mares close up in their pedigrees.

As for direct and purposeful substitution, there were rumours casting doubt on the official backgrounds of some ponies, particularly after the closing of the Inspection Scheme, and both before and after the closing of the stud books. I remember receiving an anonymous letter sent to all FPS members, back in the 1980s when the Data Protection Act hadn't been thought of and the Member list was circulated freely; it asserted that several prizewinning ponies were not what their registrations said they were, and that one was descended from a Highland.

There are two views about such substitutions. One is that it would have been fraudulent to pass off a pony as being by Stallion A when it was really by Stallion Z; but the other is that bringing in fresh bloodlines using the right stamp of pony would have been good for the health of the breed overall. For instance, I sometimes wonder whether any breeders spotted what is now known as Foal Immunodeficiency Syndrome, before it was recognised by vets, and whether they realised it could be mitigated by bringing in "something else" as an unrelated cross and applying a set of acceptable papers. But because of the fraudulent aspect, even if it was done I'm pretty sure no-one would ever have admitted to it.

And I'm sure too that there have always been less significant substitutions, such as took place thirty years ago when I bought my late driving gelding, passported as Tebay Tommy but known throughout his life as "Mr T". All parties to the purchase are now dead, except myself, so I'm not going to get into any trouble for telling this story.

Mr T was bred by Thomas Capstick, so he should have been registered as a Murthwaite pony. At the time, though, ponies could still be registered at any age, so "late" registration was common, and Mr T, still unregistered, went on loan as a young stallion to serve a herd of unregistered mares, as a trial. I conclude he didn't produce well because after a couple of seasons he was sent back and gelded. When Thomas later swapped Mr T to David Trotter in exchange for a Tebay filly, the law on registrations had been tightened: ponies had to be

Below left: Tebay Tommy a.k.a. Mr T.
His passport said he was by
Tebay Campbellton Victor (top right)
but his sire was in fact
Heltondale Hero (bottom right)

registered in their year of birth. Mr T (by then a 5 year old) found himself still unregistered, outside the stud book, and could not be shown under FPS rules. However, he was young and healthy, so David Trotter broke him to saddle and harness, and I bought him to drive.

"Do you want to show him?" David asked me. "You'll need papers, won't you, to get you into the ring for your classes. Well, I'll give you the papers from a pony we sold to that London dealer who never wants them. The pedigree on it isn't correct, it says he's by Tebay Campbellton Victor out of Tebay Diadem, but you can always ask Thomas how he's really bred. And he's a gelding, after all, so it won't matter to anybody else."

David then told me Mr T's correct pedigree, and on a separate occasion Thomas confirmed it: by Heltondale Hero out of Adamthwaite Jenny (her last foal). And I believed them, because Mr T looked like a Murthwaite pony by Heltondale Hero, not a Tebay pony by Campbellton Victor - compare them for yourself, above.

I showed Mr T for many years as a driving pony using his "official" passport as Tebay Tommy, because, no matter which sire and dam names you used to define him, he was after all pure Fell; and both his breeder and his supposed breeder were willing to let me do that, because I was getting out there and advertising the breed, and Mr T was a gelding with no registered progeny so the anomaly would never cause problems with future generations.

We wouldn't get away with it today. Registrations are much more accurate than they used to be, owing first to blood typing and then to DNA sampling, and now the fact that we microchip and register foals before the end of the year in which they are born.

The old stud books, however, are all we have got as the published pedigrees of our breed. Go with it. You just need to be aware that at some point when you are tracing a pedigree back into history, parts of it will become a paper exercise and not a record of genetic inheritance.

The further back you go, the bigger pinch of salt you'll need.

Secretaries of the Fell Pony Committee / Fell Pony Society

Pre-1922   Mr FW Garnett MRCVS
1922   Dr RW Gibson
1922   Captain Wingate
1926   Mr RB Charlton
1934   Mr J Relph
1947   Mrs S McCosh
1956   Miss P Crossland
1981   Mr C Richardson
1990   Mrs R Bell
1996   Miss S Wood
1999   Mrs J Slattery
2000   Miss C Singer
2003   Mr I Simper
2005   Mrs E Parkin
2013   Mrs K Wilkinson

I have not listed Chairmen because in the early years they were often elected for the duration of a single meeting.

Timeline of Events in Britain

19th Century
1898   First ponies registered in National Pony Society Stud Book.
1898   Description of the Fell Pony by the Fell Pony Committee for the NPS Stud Book

20th century

1914-18 World War 1

1921   Group of Fell ponies shown at London Show
1921   Stallion Premiums given annually by the Ministry of Agriculture and Fisheries
1921   Membership subscription 5 shillings per annum
1921   Society's first Fell pony sale at Kirkby Stephen Cowper Day
1921   Height of Fell ponies in future to be - Mares not exceeding 13-2 hands, Stallions not exceeding 14 hands

1921 Local inspectors appointed to inspect all animals eligible for registration and to encourage Fell Pony owners to have their ponies registered. All Stallions for registration should be passed by at least 2 members of the committee.

1922 The Fell Pony Society is officially formed.

1922 Responsibility for Stallion Premiums is transferred from Ministry of Agriculture to Light Horse Breeding Department of the War Office

1923 A pony already registered as a Fell Pony should not be transferred to the Dales Section of the NPS Stud Book (and vice versa)

1926 Foals from two registered parents will be registered, though foals from unregistered parents must be inspected before registration

1934 War Office stallion Premiums scheme withdrawn

1934 King George V buys Fell ponies and donates to the Society to make up for the War Office Premiums

1939 Grants begin to native pony breed societies by the Racecourse Betting Control Board (still continuing via the Horserace Betting Levy Board)

1939-45 World War 2

1944 & 45 Princesses Margaret and Elizabeth win show driving classes with a Fell pony at Royal Windsor

1946 Breeding Enclosures Scheme starts

1947 Updated Breed Description

1947 FPS actively encourages the registration of stock post-war who would otherwise be lost to the stud book due to the 1926 ruling

1953 Short promotional Film planned

1954 FPS adopts the Fell pony logo drawn for Ponies of Britain by Deane Skurray

1960 Fell ponies carry "Early Britons" in a historical display at the International Horse Show at White City, London

1966 Rules drawn up including updated Breed Standard

1961 Letters IS to be added to registration numbers of Inspected Stock, resulting generations to carry A, then B; 3rd generation considered pure Fell, with no extra letters in the registration number

1965 Colts from Inspected mares (IS, A, B) to be gelded before registration

1966-68 First volume of the Fell Pony News

1966-1974 (revised 1981) Height limit for mares and stallions is 14 hands plus half an inch for shoes.

1969 First FPS publicity leaflet

1969 Stud Book closes; ponies can only be accepted from 2 registered Fell pony parents

1970 HRH Prince Philip begins driving a team of Fell ponies in competitive driving trials

1970 First Summer Breed Show

1971 Trainee Judges Scheme begins

1973 Breeding Enclosures reduced to one only

1978 Molly Laing and Twislehope Rex represent the Fells in a Musical Ride at Wembley (Mrs Laing subsequently organised other displays by Fell ponies at big southern shows)

1979 Fell ponies take part in a historical pageant during Lowther Horse Driving Trials

1980 FPS begins managing its own Stud Book

1980 Half-yearly FPS Newsletter starts

1980 Performance Trials begin (Packway; Blawith; later at Linnel Wood)

1982 HM The Queen graciously agrees to become Patron of the FPS

1983 First FPS-issued stallion licence (Townend Duke III)

1987 HRH Princess Anne rides a Fell pony in Holyrood Park, Edinburgh

1988 HRH Princess Diana meets a Fell at the Royal Show

1989 First Southern Breed Show

1993 Stallions and colts to be blood-typed before licensing

1993 All ponies to be registered in their year of birth

1995 Foal Immunodeficiency Syndrome (FIS) brought to vets' attention by Paul May MRCVS

1995 Daughter Society formed in the Netherlands

1996 Liverpool University begins research at Leahurst into FIS

1996 FPS incorporates to Limited Company status; Memorandum and Articles of Association written

1998 Equine passports introduced

1999 Voluntary DNA sampling of stallions (later compulsory before licensing)

1999 HM The Queen visits Lowther Horse Driving Trials and watches the Fell pony show classes

21st Century

2000 1st version of the FPS Web site built

2000 Area Support Groups formed

2000 Optional microchipping of Filly foals (compulsory by 2002)

2003 Postal voting for General Meetings introduced

2004 FPS is registered as a Charity

2004 Overseas Branches are recognised in USA and Europe

2005 All equines must have a passport

2007 The FPS Newsletter becomes the FPS Magazine

2009 Learning with Fells educational scheme begins

2009 First FPS 'Press Officer' appointed

2010 FIS carrier test is announced by Liverpool University and available to breeders

2014   Young Persons Group (YPG) formed

2015   FPS Display Team formed

2016   135 Fell ponies form a Guard of Honour to HM the Queen at Windsor for her 90th Birthday

2018   Lady Louise Windsor drives a Fell Pony pair at Windsor Horse Show

2019   Microchipping becomes compulsory for all equines

2021   "Brexit" creates problems with registering EU-born foals through the UK mother studbook

2021   Daughter Society formed in Denmark

2021   Young Persons Group re-forms as the Next Generation Group

2021   HRH Princess Anne visits Westmorland County Show and requests to meet the Fell Pony Society's Display Team

2022

2022   The Society celebrates its 100th year:

Launch at Royal Windsor Horse Show to celebrate the Society's 100 years,

HM The Queen's Platinum Jubilee of 70 years, and

her 40 years of patronage of the Society

Launch at the Stallion Show at Dalemain:

Parade of past champions

Performance by the Display Team

Centenary Pennant starts journey round UK Area Support Groups

Photo shoot of the day's events

Educational Video, "Type & Conformation"

This book

International Standard Serial Number (ISSN) applied to the FPS Magazine from the Centenary issue onward

"100 Miles with a Fell Pony" Challenge taken up by hundreds of owners in UK, Europe and North America

The Breed Show

Art Exhibition, Talks, Workshops, at the Old Courthouse, Shap

Stud visits and rides

Centenary Ball at Kendal

Death of the Society's Patron HM Queen Elizabeth II

The Society awaits news of its future Patron, not yet announced (December)

Timeline of Events in North America
compiled by Victoria Tollman

pre-1934 A stallion by Dalesman is sold to a buyer in Michigan, along with 5 Fell mares.

1934 Roy Charlton exports 3 mares to the Mackay-Smiths' Farnley Farm in Virginia, and a stallion to a buyer in South Carolina. The mares are put to non-Fell pony stallions.

1940 Franklyn L Hutton owns 15 "Feld" ponies in Charleston, South Carolina.

1952 the Mackay-Smiths travel to Cumbria and purchase Dalemain Bluebell, as a child's pony; she and D. Foxglove work as shooting ponies in Louisiana.

mid-1950s – E.P. Taylor (Windfield Farms, breeder of 1962 Derby winner Northern Dancer) imports Fell mares & 2 stallions to supplement his racing stable broodmare operation. All resulting colts are gelded and sold, fillies are either sold or retained to become nurse mares to Thoroughbred foals.

mid-1950s – Howard S. Mitchell imports registered Fell stock. Details unknown.

1988-1999 – Lyle & Mary Nygaard (Newfarm, retired) import 3 stallions and 3 mares to Florida; Newfarm Valencia, f.1993, is the 1st Fell foal in North America to be registered.

1993-1999 – Carolyn Sharp Handeland (Midnightvalley, retired) of Colorado, imports 1 grey stallion and 2 black mares; 1st foal born in 1994.

1996 Victoria Tollman (BroughHill), North Carolina; 1999 1st foal – BroughHill Hadrian's Wall, 2020 most recent BroughHill foal.

1997 Newfarm Midsummers Night is 1st Licensed USA-bred Fell stallion; at stud at BroughHill Fells in Florida.

1999 Fell Pony Society & Conservancy of the Americas is founded, including 95% of all known North American Fell owners & breeders at the time

1999-2005 "Fell Pony Journal" – NA Fell pony hardcopy publication with international circulation, including HM the Queen by her request. Editor: Victoria Tollman

2000 Mary Jean Gould-Earley (Laurelhighland) of Pennsylvania, purchases several Fell ponies when Newfarm retire; 1st foal Laurelhighland Knight Waver, 2000

2000 Equitana – Debut exhibit of Fell Pony breed (over 100,000 spectators) by Fell Pony Society & Conservancy of the Americas & Mary Jean Gould-Earley, Pennsylvania

2000 Newfarm Midsummers Night becomes 1st Fell pony stallion anywhere to produce foals by A.I. (both coolcd & frozcn)

2000 1st DNA Fell Pony study (40 ponies) by Dr. Gus Cothran, University of Kentucky

2002 Fell Pony Society of North America is founded; 1st issue of their "Fell Pony Express". Editor: Mary Jean Gould-Earley

2003 NA population = 70 imports plus live births more than doubled Fell numbers

2003 the world famous Kentucky Horse Park (KHP), Lexington, with annual visitation of over 500,000 annually, organises a seasonal breed display including Fell gelding Hardendale Black Jack, loaned by Laura Hart

2003 British Rare Breeds On Parade at KHP – exhibition & 1st sanctioned M&M show organized by Victoria Tollman (BroughHill Fells); judges Clive Richardson and Sue Millard (UK)

2003 Equine Affaire, New England – Fell Pony Society of North America exhibit with booth & breed demonstrations, first of many years

2004 1st Dressage at Devon M&M in-hand class, organized by Mary Jean Gould-Earley (Laurelhighland Fells).

2004 Two official Overseas Support Groups approved by FPS
 – Fell Pony Society of North America
 – Fell Pony Society & Conservancy of the Americas

2004 Equine Affaire, New England – Fell Pony Society & Conservancy co-partners with the Equus Survival Trust, first of many years, with a booth & display demonstrations.

2008 1st NA Fell Pony Nationals – hosted by the Fell Pony Society & Conservancy, supported with FPS rosettes in partnership with the Equus Survival Trust

2011 NA Fell Pony census records over 350 registered ponies

2012 Fells invited to display for Breyerfest; attracts 30,000 spectators at the KHP, Lexington

2014 Breyerfest features Fell ponies on exhibition, supported by Conservancy members Heather Kyle (ScafellPike, Kentucky) and Allison Wolfe. Breyer showcase a revised Breyer model, originally based on Mary Jean Gould-Earley's stallion Waverhead Model IV, and renamed as Carltonlima Emma, the trusted mount of HRH Queen Elizabeth II; a percentage of sales goes to the FPS each quarter thereafter.

2017 NA Fell population reaches 600 registered ponies

2019 Beverly Patrick's 4-in-hand Fell Pony team wins the American Driving Society's Preliminary Pony Team Championship at Metamora, Michigan

2020 NA Fell population = almost 700 registered ponies.

2021 Fell pony on loan to the KHP from owner Heather Kyle (Scafellpike) for seasonal display at the Breeds Barn promoting the Fell breed in their daily exhibitions.

Congratulations from the Fell Pony Society of the Netherlands

On behalf of the NFPS, we would like to congratulate the FPS by achieving such a great accomplishment.

Throughout the years we have been very privileged to be able to purchase beautiful Fell ponies from the UK, which also provided us the possibility to create the wonderful Fell pony population we currently have in the Netherlands.

We managed to create our own breeding and judging system, by keeping in mind and respecting both FPS as well as national rules and regulations. For instance, we have been able to create a large DNA pool and have insight in inbreeding coefficients and stallion lines. We organize yearly stallion- and breed-shows, using experienced judges who have judged with FPS judges in the past as well.

We've always appreciated our warm contacts with both the FPS council and judges, as well as the UK breeders and we are looking forward to continuing in the future!

Met vriendelijke groet,

Joyce de Hoogh, Stamboeksecretaris NFPS

Timeline of Events in Europe and elsewhere

1927   Stallions eg Linnel Glen, Wait and See, Blencathra, Jack's Delight, Wallthwaite Ranger, exported, in particular to northern Spain, to breed military packhorses

1948   Linnel Sandpiper exported to Australia

1948   Stallions, eg, Dalemain Knight of the Thistle, exported to Pakistan, to breed military packhorses

1950   Dalemain Roamer exported to France

1951   International Pony Breeders' Federation founded in Koln, Germany

1979   Fell pony doing dressage in Sweden

1988   Fell ponies exported to France, Najac stud

1992   Fell pony registrations in Germany, eg Mrs Muller's Narnia stud

1994   Fell pony registrations in The Netherlands, eg Mr Ottink's Wildhoeve stud

1995   Society founded in The Netherlands - Mr GH Ottink chairman, Mrs MHM Weegerink secretary

1996   First Annual Breed show in The Netherlands

1997   Nederlands Fellpony Stamboek (NFPS) officially recognised as daughter society by the FPS

1999   1st NFPS stallion license awarded to a Dutch-bred stallion (Wildhoeve Boy)

2000   100th Fell pony foal born/registered in the Netherlands

2004   Fell Pony Society Branch groups formed in Denmark and France; Contacts to represent owners of Fells in Belgium, South Germany and Switzerland

2004   Fell ponies bred and registered in Czech Republic

2005   Celebration of 10 years by NFPS

2008   Fell ponies bred and registered in Australia

2010   First geldings entering the annual NFPS breed show

2012   Fell ponies sold from Czech Republic to Russia

2016   First Fell pony Sport day in the Netherlands

2016   First 'Sport' titles awarded by NFPS to ponies performing successfully in either riding or driving competitions

2019   First championship for geldings awarded by NFPS (won by Knillis van het Westerkwartier)

2021   Fell Pony Society Branch formed in Sweden

2021   Daughter Society formed in Denmark

2022   NFPS celebrates being an official daughter society of the FPS for 25 years

WHERE DO WE GO FROM HERE?

Sue Millard

Matters from the Past

The Fell Pony Society office is in Appleby, and HM The Queen has been its patron since 1982. The FPS is the official UK passport-issuing authority, registering ponies from the UK and worldwide. It is the main source of data about the breed for DEFRA, the Rare Breeds Survival Trust and other organisations.

The Society spent a lot of energy in its early years just getting Fell ponies in the district recognised and registered. It was only when a farm had a good year that people spent money registering ponies, so often a mare, her daughters and her grand-daughters were all registered at the same time. Now, the Stud Book is closed and both parents have to be registered in order for a foal to have a FPS passport. DNA sampling and microchipping ensure that parentage is correct.

FPS has Branches in Europe and North America to help owners overseas, and runs training days for potential pony judges.

The Foal Immunodeficiency Syndrome that was recognised in 1995 (in other breeds, not just Fells) is under control through genetic marker testing provided by Liverpool University in 2010, and we still have a broader and healthier gene pool, with more ancient DNA, than one might expect from the data in the Stud Book (Winton, 2020).

Concerns for the Future

Now that the UK has left the European Union and the Single Market, the Society is liaising with other pedigree breed societies in the UK who are all still trying to untangle the bureaucratic difficulties of registering British breeds if they are born in the EU.

Changes in Government policies and decreasing profits in farming may adversely affect the herds of ponies in the hill country. While there is certainly a case for reducing stock numbers if the ground is overstocked, overgrazed or otherwise depleted, there is also a case to be made to defend the hill farmers who have used the common for generations; not only for ponies but for the farmed livestock that go into the food chain. The current push for "re-wilding" must not be allowed to remove the rights of farms to run their ponies on the commons, because these semi wild herds are the hardy nucleus of the breed.

Fell ponies and the farmers who are their breeders are as much a part of Cumbrian history and ecology as the Herdwick sheep. The Society continues to run a "Learning with Fells" scheme for its members to emphasise the importance of the hill herds for the long-term health of the breed. The FPS joins in meetings about Commons management and discussions of new legislation, and has a Conservation and Grazing sub-committee that gathers data to be used in support of the breed as well as helping to match ponies to conservation site requirements.

The Fell pony breed has had nationwide publicity over the years, for example on Countryfile and the old Dales Diary, and Rare Steeds (Radio 4) and the FPS hopes to get more media attention in May 2022 with the Centenary launches at Windsor and at Dalemain.

The Commons

There is a current trend to reduce Government support for farmers, and the risk to the Fell pony breed is that it will ignore the traditional hill farmers who are the backbone of the hill-bred herds. While Cumbria Commoners are fighting on the farmers' behalf, especially during the pilot stages of the Environmental Land Management Scheme, we also have to make sure the Fell pony is included in those considerations, and try to prevent adverse decisions being made.

Shouldn't the value that we are placing on trees and wildlife be balanced by the value of the community that lives locally and uses the land in traditional ways with local livestock? I'm reading James Rebanks' *English Pastoral* and agree with him that there is a lot to be said for retaining traditional mixed farming practices because they involve many, varied ways of keeping the land healthy and the food worth eating. It is the people themselves who are a resource of knowledge and diverse skills that can be resilient in the face of changing climate.

Over such wide areas of grassland as a fell common, the sheep and deer, rabbits and hares, cattle and horses all graze in different ways and produce different sward patterns. We have probably seen too many sheep on the fell in the last fifty years, but removing them completely, or replacing them entirely with cattle, seems unnecessarily drastic. It's the mix of grazers, moving to fresh ground regularly, that keeps parasites at a low level and provides habitats for the widest range of wild plants, invertebrates, birds and mammals. If the hill farms ever lose the rights to run ponies on high fell commons, the Fells can only keep their hardy nucleus if breeders have enough space on to graze them on allotments, intakes and rough corners of the farm; or else they will change, slowly but surely, into a softer, more lowland breed.

Collective vs Individual Preferences

A hill farm having rights to graze ponies on the fell is a small but important contribution to the make-up of the Fell pony breed. However, environmental land management and "rewilding" are high-level concerns on which any one individual can have only a limited amount of impact. In compiling this book I have seen over and over again how Fell pony breeders, individually and together, have taken hold of what they have inherited, kept some aspects and discarded others.

Let me put forward a specific example from the past - the filly Ousel 2891, on the following page. She was bred in 1908 by Henry Holme of Thrimby, north of Shap, sired by Dalesman 572 out of 2249 Flora III. Both ponies are in all our stock today, along with many others featured in this book, and many that I haven't had space to mention at all.

Now, Ousel was registered in the Fell section of the NPS stud book, as was her dam, presumably reflecting the NPS concept of "a pony from the Fell country suitable to breed riding or polo ponies" rather than the local view of what was typical Fell stock. She was described as piebald, a colour pattern no longer admitted by the Society in the Main section of the Stud Book, and she was nowhere near the image of today's typical pony. She stood 13.3½ hands - well above the 13.2hh height limit for Fell mares which was imposed ten years after she was registered, a limit which lasted for 40+ years. If Ousel did not have the groom standing beside her to give scale, this photograph could easily be a modern Clydesdale-cross of 15 hands or more. So what are we looking at here?

This is a pony that belonged to an influential man. He was president of the Fell Pony Committee, and later of the Society. He had liked the dam, Flora III, well enough to buy back not only Ousel but her full sisters Hoopoe and Swallow. He also owned at least one other mare that would not now be permitted in the Main section, the chestnut 3763 Shrike.

However, the majority of breeders in the formative years of the Society were breeding and registering solid-coloured blacks, browns, greys and bays with few white markings, and eventually they chose to make those the only acceptable colours. This is a very clear demonstration of membership power. Collectively, the owners and breeders decided over the years what a Fell pony should look like. The piebald and chestnut ponies that Lord Lonsdale bought and registered as Fells would now be placed in Section X.

"Permissible colours", of course, are limited and fairly obvious, whereas type and conformation require a much more discriminating eye. Look at Ousel's shape compared to a modern mare - Heltondale Maydew VII, Border Black Empress, Lunesdale Lucky Lady, Lunesdale Rebecca, Bewcastle Blossom. Compared to a mid-century mare, even compared to

One of Mighty Atom's grandchildren - Ousel 2891 foaled 1908; by Dalesman 572 out of 2249 Flora III. The annotation says, "This photo could make quite a talking point! Ousel is in the 'Black Book' on page 34 and registered as 'piebald'. The comment on the back of the original photo in Grandpa Roy's handwriting is 'What a shame of Lord Lonsdale the "Circus Man".' The Yellow Earl owned this pony and we believe this photo was taken at his residence in Rutland." Perhaps the "white face and hind legs" of her dam Flora may have been markings like these. Photo, Charlton Collection

her 1930s relative Linnel Flighty, she is a different shape and type: because of the choices made since then by the majority of Fell pony breeders, to please themselves and their buyers.

This is what a breed society does. Members collaborate, they reach a consensus about their preferences, then they select stock and impose those preferences on them. Although a nucleus of Fell ponies still run free today on the commons (and long may they do so) even there they do not have the freedom of choice that truly wild animals have in their mating. They have no choice about what their descendants will be like. Those of us who own them control the matings, and the identity of the breed in the future.

You may be able to see, by studying the generously donated photographs which I have been able to publish here, that the ponies of the last 50 years are subtly different from those of the preceding 50 years. There have been distinct changes, not only of permitted colours, but of shape and type and hairiness and possibly of hardiness, and they have made the modern Fell pony quite different from the filly Ousel, even though the genes of her sire Dalesman and and her dam Flora III exist in every animal.

There are some changes that have been imposed by other challenges: for example, dealing with a legacy from the 1950s and '60s in the form of FIS; but many others stem from individual choices rather than from the demands of farming or commercial work. Ponies in 2022 are a luxury, not a necessity, we no longer test their mettle with daily work at the level that was seen in the 19th and early 20th centuries, and less than half of the annual foal crop is born in a hill-going herd. Environmental pressures and epigenetic effects are biased towards a lowland expression of their genes.

Horse ownership is still a strong leisure area, and there is a huge industry based on it, providing feed, bedding, tack, harness, clothing, vehicles, horseboxes and medicines. Some aspects of this "leisure pony" may have improved but there are faults, even in prizewinning animals, that were not there 50 years ago. Feather is sometimes cited as a major change, but to me that is neither here nor there; you could clip it off and a stabled pony that is working and not being shown would be none the worse for it. The same cannot be said for poor conformation such as upright shoulders, narrow or long backs or weak quarters, which should not be passed as correct but sometimes are; while round bone, narrow feet or too-straight hocks can be obscured by heavy feather, full manes and tails, and the modern "hands off" approach to show judging. If you want to learn more about good Fell pony type and conformation, watch the FPS video that Tom Lloyd has produced for the Society in 2022.

Just as current breeders have had to work with the inheritance of the past century, the breeding decisions they make now will affect what the younger Fell pony owners have to work with in the future. The choices people make today will influence the breed next year and the next, and what their inheritors will breed beyond that. The choices that judges make in the show ring can influence new owners and potential owners. What you want a pony for, as a buyer, can influence what breeders keep to breed from and what they sell. What you do in public with your pony, at shows and events, can influence what other buyers want to buy, and again, what breeders keep and what they sell.

Whether you are an owner, an exhibitor, a judge or a breeder, I hope that this gives you further reasons to pause and consider what you will do with the ponies you own, show, judge or breed. We must make sure that what we do will be worthy of the last 100 years and remain a good foundation for the next century.

REFERENCES & FURTHER READING

BEAMISH MUSEUM: Beamish People's Collection, *http://collections.beamish.org.uk/* January 2022.

BIBBY, M A, in Horse Breeds and Human Society: Purity, Identity and the Making of the Modern Horse, Edited By Kristen Guest, Monica Mattfeld, 2019: "How northern was Pistol? The Galloway nag as self-identity and satire in an age of supra-national horse trading." pp 69-85. (London, Routledge); also personal correspondence 2021-2022.

BOWER MA, Campana MG, Whitten M, et al. The cosmopolitan maternal heritage of the Thoroughbred racehorse breed shows a significant contribution from British and Irish native mares. Biol Lett. 2011;7(2):316-320. doi:10.1098/rsbl.2010.0800.

BRITISH NEWSPAPER ARCHIVE, *https://www.britishnewspaperarchive.co.uk/* accessed January 2022.

CARTER S D, FOX-CLIPSHAM L Y, CHRISTLEY R, SWINBURNE J, Foal immunodeficiency syndrome: carrier testing has markedly reduced disease incidence. Veterinary Record, April 2013. *https://bvajournals.onlinelibrary.wiley.com/doi/10.1136/vr.101451* Accessed February 2022.

CHARLTON, R B, 1952 edition: A Lifetime with Ponies. London, Hodder & Stoughton.

CHARLTON COLLECTION: private collection of papers and photographs from RB Charlton and his family.

DAVIES, R. W. The Supply of Animals to the Roman Army and the Remount System. Latomus, vol. 28, no. 2, 1969, pp. 429–459. JSTOR, *www.jstor.org/stable/41527450.* Accessed 21 July 2021.

DEFOE, D, 1724 - 1727: A Tour Through the Whole Island of Great Britain, Letter XXI, cited in Dent, 1962: A History of British Native Ponies, p170.

DONALDSON, G, 1942: The Attitude of Whitgift and Bancroft to the Scottish Church, *https://www.jstor.org/stable/3678470.* Accessed May 2022.

FELL PONY SOCIETY History CD 2002: digital archive of press cuttings, stud cards, notebooks and sales notices, mainly from Mr R B Charlton.

FELL PONY SOCIETY, 1980: Stud Book 1898-1980. FPS, Penrith, Cumbria.

FELL PONY SOCIETY, 2022: Grassroots stud data. *https://breeds.grassroots.co.uk/Auth/Login?BreedCode=FELL* (accessible to FPS members)

FELL PONY SOCIETY web site, FIS Breeding Combinations, *http://www.fellponysociety.org.uk/Docs/2016%20FIS%20-%20Different%20breeding%20combinations%20and%20possible%20outcomes.doc*

FELL PONY SOCIETY Archives, Cumbria County Archives, Kendal, Cumbria.

FELL PONY SOCIETY Web site, *http://www.fellponysociety.org.uk* 2022.

FELL PONY SOCIETY MAGAZINE (formerly NEWSLETTER and NEWS), ISSNs applied for. FPS Office, Bank House, Boroughgate, Appleby, Cumbria CA16 6XF. Online back copies, *http://www.fellponysociety.org.uk/newsletters.htm* 2022.

FITZGERALD, I, 2000: Dales Ponies. Suffolk: Whittet Books.

GAFFNEY, V., THOMSON K., FINCH S., 2007: Mapping Doggerland: The Mesolithic Landscapes of the Southern North Sea. Archaeopress Publishing Ltd.

GARNETT, F W, 1912: Westmorland Agriculture 1800-1900.

GIBBARD, P, 2007: How Britain Became an Island. *https://core.ac.uk/download/pdf/287522.pdf* accessed February 2022

GOULD-EARLEY, Dr. M J, 2004: The Fell Pony Family Album.

HARDIMAN, J R, The Thoroughbred Racehorse, Confused Pedigrees And Mistaken Identities. *http://www.highflyer.supanet.com/investigation2.htm* Accessed June 2003/11 December 2013.

LOW, D, 1846: On the domesticated animals of the British islands. London: Longman, Brown, Green & Longmans.

LUDWIG A, Pruvost M, Reissmann M, et al, 2009: Coat color variation at the beginning of horse domestication. Science. 2009;324(5926):485. doi:10.1126/science.1172750

MARKHAM G, 1660: The Horseman's Honour or The Beautie of Horsemanship.

MARON DF, 2014: Diet during Pregnancy Linked to Diabetes in Grandchildren. USA, Scientific American.

MILLARD, S, 2001-2022: The Fell Pony and Countryside Museums at Dalemain, *http://www.fellponymuseum.org.uk*

MILLARD, S, 2005: Hoofprints in Eden, Hayloft Books (2nd print edition by Jackdaw E Books 2018).

MORLAND, A W, 1995: A Lifetime in the Fells. Kirkby Stephen, Cerberus (printers).

MORRISSEY, J, 2021: Fell Pony Observations, Vol 2. USA: Morrissey.

MURRAY, D A, 2005: The Fell Pony: grazing characteristics and breed profile – a preliminary assessment. A feasibility study on the potential role of Fell ponies in conservation grazing post Common Agricultural Policy reform. MATILDA, Leicester, UK. *http://www.scribd.com/doc/68471432/Semi-Feral-Fell-Pony-Report* Accessed 10 Dec 2013.

PAST PRESENTED, Cumberland Chronicle or Whitehaven Intelligencer, *http://www.pastpresented.info/index.htm* Accessed 11 November 2004/11 December 2013.

PRINGLE, A, 1794: A General View of the Agriculture of the County of Westmorland. Board of Agriculture, later the Royal Agricultural Society. In MARSHALL, W, 1808: A review of the reports to the Board of Agriculture from the northern department of England: comprizing Northumberland, Durham, Cumberland, Westmoreland, Lancashire, Yorkshire; and the mountainous parts of Derbyshire, &c; Board of Agriculture. London : Longman, Hurst, Rees, and Orme, *https://archive.org/details/reviewofreportst00mars* Accessed February 2022.

RICHARDSON, C, 1990: The Fell Pony. London: J A Allen.

RICHARDSON, C, 1995: The Hackney. London: J A Allen.

SMITH, Rev S, 1810: General View of the Agriculture of Galloway, available from The Internet Archive, *https://archive.org/details/bub_gb_482OqSbqoxwC*, Accessed January 2022.

THOMAS, G, BELL S C, PHYTHIAN C, June 2003: Aid to the antemortem diagnosis of Fell pony foal syndrome by the analysis of B lymphocytes, The Veterinary Record 152(20):618-21.

VINDOLANDA Tablets Online *http://vindolanda.csad.ox.ac.uk/tablets/* December 2021.

VIRGIL, Georgics: *https://www.loebclassics.com/view/virgil-georgics/1916/pb_LCL063.181.xml* February 2022.

WINTON, C L, et al., 2020: Genetic diversity within and between British and Irish breeds: The maternal and paternal history of native ponies, in Ecology and Evolution (John Wiley & Sons) Ltd.https://onlinelibrary.wiley.com/doi/full/10.1002/ece3.5989. October 2020.

YOUATT, W, 1831: The Horse (4th ed, 1908). London: Longmans, Green & Co.

To find more information about Fell ponies see the breed society web site *www.fellponysociety.org.uk* or the Facebook page *www.facebook.com/fellponysocietyUK*. Social media presence also includes YouTube, Twitter and Instagram.

References for Commons article, p101

i   Peter Fowler, 2002, Farming in the First Millennium AD, p59.

ii   Cumberland & Westmorland Herald June 2003, reviewing Ian Whyte, 2003, Transforming Fell and Valley, Centre for North West Regional Studies. https://www.cwherald.com/a/archive/cumbrian-countryside-created-by-enclosures.254471.html

iii   Ian Whyte, Parliamentary enclosure and changes in landownership in an upland environment: Westmorland, c.1770–1860. https://www.bahs.org.uk/AGHR/ARTICLES/54n2a4.pdf

iv   DEFRA Database of Common Land, published 2012, dataset dated 1993. https://assets.publishing.service.gov.uk/government/uploads/system/uploads/attachment_data/file/572998/common-land.xls

v   Government Guidance on Managing Common Land, June 2015. https://www.gov.uk/guidance/managing-common-land

vi   Countryside and Rights of Way Act 2000, http://www.legislation.gov.uk/ukpga/2000/37/contents

vii Cumbria County Council, Commons Registration Service https://www.cumbria.gov.uk/planning-environment/conservation/commons-registration-service/

viii Lancashire County Council, Commons Registration Service, https://www.lancashire.gov.uk/council/transparency/registers/commons-register/

ix   Federation of Cumbria Commoners, Map of Cumbria's Commons, http://www.cumbriacommoners.org.uk/cumbria-commons-map

x   DEFRA Database of Common Land, 2012. As above.

xi   Commons Register 2000, https://datacac.uk/csvTable/united-kingdom/Commons-register-England,--2000-26.html

xii Basic Payment Scheme subsidies (Common Land Grazing Rights 2017), https://assets.publishing.service.gov.uk/government/uploads/system/uploads/attachment_data/file/698817/Common_land_grazing_rights_Final_2017.pdf

xiii Basic Payment Scheme Rules 2018. https://assets.publishing.service.gov.uk/government/uploads/system/uploads/attachment_data/file/705756/BPS_2018_scheme_rules_v5.0.pdf

xiv Commons eligibility checks 2019, https://www.gov.uk/government/publications/commons-eligibility-checks

xv   Basic Payment Scheme Rules 2018. As above.

xvi Government Guidance on Managing Common Land, June 2015. As above.

xvii Government Guidance on Managing Common Land, June 2015. As above.

xviii Government Guidance on Managing Common Land, June 2015. As above.

xix FPS Council Minutes, July 2018.

xx   FPS Stud Book entries 2015-2021. The Grassroots online database carries current data from all Fell registrations received from the UK and worldwide, apart from the two Daughter Societies (Netherlands and Denmark) which are printed by agreement in the annual issues of the FPS Stud Book.

xxi FPS data in Grassroots database, accessible from the FPS web site if you are a Society member.

xxii The Guardian, September 2018. https://www.theguardian.com/uk-news/2018/sep/14/cumbria-villagers-oppose-army-bid-to-grab-common-land

xxiii Cumberland & Westmorland Herald, 31 August 2019.

https://www.nationalarchives.gov.uk/help-with-your-research/research-guides/manorial-documents-lordships-how-to-use-manorial-document-register/

https://www.nationalarchives.gov.uk/help-with-your-research/research-guides/common-lands/

Acknowledgments

I am very grateful to the many people who so generously enabled the use of photographs, articles and background information, including:

Fell Pony Society Archives, web site & Magazine; Cumbria Archive Centre, Kendal; Barbara Bell; Sarah Charlton & her family's collection of photographs; the Beamish People's Collection; John Cockbain; Michael Goddard; Jean Jackson & Shap History Society Archive; Anna Metcalfe; Sharron Gibson Metcalfe; Christine Morton; Bert Morland; Jenifer Morrissey; Greta Noble; Bill Potter; Penny Randell; Clive Richardson; Victoria Tollman; Betty Walker; Eileen Walker; Liz Whitley; Katherine Wilkinson; Janet Wood; Julia Woods; and photographers including Ruth Eastwood; Joanne Bennett; Jo Exley; JP Event Photography; Anthony Reynolds; Claire Simpson.

I know that I will have missed thanking some of my many contributors - for which I apologise in advance and assure you that I am, nonetheless, grateful for your generosity.

Sue Millard driving FP2681 Coppyhill Suzanne f.1995, AKA Ruby, by Heltondale Ted FP487C out of FP1339 Sleddale Holly. Grandsire Lunesdale Jerry 4745, grand-dam 12443 Sleddale Dainty XIII by Sleddale King of the Fell 5902. Ruby had two foals for her previous owner Alison O'Neill, by Waverhead Prince II and Murthwaite Bross. Photo, the-Event-Photographer

Also by Sue Millard

About Fell ponies and other horses, and their people

Hoofprints in Eden *(non fiction)*

Ponies with Wheels *(non fiction)*

Horses in the Garden *(non fiction)*

Against the Odds *(novel)*

Scratch *(novel, sequel to Against the Odds)*

Coachman *(historical novel)*

String of Horses *(novel)*

One Fell Swoop *(cartoons)*

Fell Facts / Fell Fun *(activity books for children)*

Other books

The Forthright Saga *(novella)*

Dragon Bait *(novella)*

Ash Tree *(poetry)*

Ruby Wedding *(poetry)*

Galloway Gate *(poetry)*

Keeping On *(short stories)*

The Twisted Stair *(short stories)*

www.jackdawebooks.co.uk

About the Author

Sue Millard lives in Greenholme, Cumbria, in the heart of Fell pony country. She has been a fan of the breed for 50 years, having first met them when she worked at a hotel with a trekking stable and breeding stud, and she has subsequently ridden and driven many miles with (mostly brown) Fell ponies.

She has served on the FPS Council since 2005. She has been the FPS Webmaster since 2012 and Magazine Editor since 2008, and she has scripted and commentated for the FPS Display Team since 2015.

She also writes novels, non-fiction and poetry.

Her previous major work on Fells, *Hoofprints in Eden*, won the Saint & Co prize in the Lake District Book of the Year Awards in 2006.

Online:

Web site: https://www.jackdawebooks.co.uk
Facebook: https://www.facebook.com/JackdawEBooks
Instagram: https://www.instagram.com/fellponycumbria/

Reviews of Hoofprints in Eden (2005)

' The Duke of Edinburgh's office, at
        Buckingham Palace, has just ordered
        three copies...' Cumberland &
        Westmorland Herald, 2005

'Studying Sue's book, I can see how the ponies
        of the fell define and fulfil a way of life.'
        Simon Baddeley, April 2020.

'...something exceptional here - a book that
        offers the reader an experience that is
        close to an oral history recording...'
        HorsebackHistorian, 4 Nov 2013

'Sue Millard has written the definitive account
        of the breed...' Steve Matthews,
        Bookcase / BooksCumbria, Carlisle
        2005

Printed in Great Britain
by Amazon

13237256R00127